RSI:
The Complete Guide

Traders Press, Inc.®
PO Box 6206
Greenville, SC 29606

John Hayden

ISBN: 0-934380-88-0
Published by Traders Press, Inc.®

This publication is designed to provide accurate and authoritative information with regard to the subject matter covered. It is sold with the understanding that the publisher is not engaged in rendering legal, accounting, or other professional advice. If legal advice or other expert assistance is required, the services of a competent professional person should be sought.

Editing by: Roger Reimer
&
Teresa Darty Alligood
Layout and Cover Design by: Teresa Alligood
Traders Press, Inc.®

Traders Press, Inc.®
PO Box 6206
Greenville, SC 29606

Books and Gifts
for Investors and Traders

DEDICATION

I would like to dedicate this book to the one person who has inspired me the most to live my life to the best of my ability. This is my wonderful wife, Valeriya Hayden.

ACKNOWLEDGEMENTS

In the preparation and the writing of this book there were many people who contributed, inspired, and encouraged my efforts in placing these thoughts onto paper. Additionally there are many people that have guided me in my efforts in becoming a better trader. I would particularly like to express my gratitude to my wife Valeriya Hayden for patience and encouragement, Christopher Castroviejo whose mentoring was crucial in my understanding of time analysis and the "big picture", and Andrew Cardwell who taught in his seminars of the early 1990's some of the concepts mentioned in this book.

SPECIAL THANKS

Creating this manuscript was made possible with the help of three individuals. I would like to take this opportunity to thank my wife, Valeriya Hayden, who has supported me in countless ways. I would also like to thank Joe Schedlbauer, who was invaluable in critiquing the ideas that this manuscript encompasses. And finally, I would like to thank Edward Dobson. His unfailing encouragement helped me complete the writing of this comprehensive book about the RSI. Without this encouragement, this manuscript would never have been born. Thank you.

A book only comes "alive" when the reader becomes involved with the subject matter. I would like to take this opportunity to say "Thank you" to the readers of this book for taking their valuable time to learn more about truly understanding price behavior.

Table of Contents

Table of Contents

The Complete RSI Book

Charting Table of Contents

"In trading, as in life, what often appears obvious is not important and what is not obvious is important." – John Hayden

SECTION I

PREPARATION AND UNDERSTANDING – THE KEY TO SUCCESS!

CHAPTER 1

OVERVIEW

In the "old" pre-personal computer days, bar charts and indicator values had to be calculated and plotted by hand on honest-to-goodness paper charts. It was during this 'early' time that the Relative Strength Index or RSI first made its appearance.

In June 1978, Welles Wilder introduced the Relative Strength Index to the trading community in an article for *Commodities Magazine*. In his classic book, *"New Concepts in Technical Trading Systems,"* Mr. Wilder provided step-by-step instructions on calculating and interpreting the Relative Strength Index. As time has passed, other indicators with similar sounding names have been developed. The majority of traders refer to this index as the "RSI" instead of the "Relative Strength Index." This helps to avoid confusion with other indicators with similar names. For example, *Investor's Business Daily* publishes its "Relative Strength Rankings" and John Murphy promotes his "Relative Strength Charts." Neither of these 'relative strength tools' is related to Welles Wilder's Relative Strength Index or RSI, as we shall call it.

The Relative Strength Index (RSI) is one of the most popular momentum oscillators used by traders. It is so popular that every charting software package and professional trading system anywhere in the world has it as one of its primary indicators. Not only is this indicator included in every charting package, but it is not out of the realm of possibility that every system has identical original default settings.

There are many reasons that the Relative Strength Index quickly became so popular with traders. When hand plotted in conjunction with a daily bar chart, it provided interpretative information on market tops and bottoms, chart formations, market reversals, areas of support/resistance, and price/indicator divergence. All of this information was rolled into one easy to calculate formula, so what was not to like? At this time, enter the personal computer bringing with it the ability to manipulate numbers in the blink of an eye. The personal computer has made the process of decision-making so easy with instant real-time charts and indicator overlays that most traders simply do not know where to begin.

It is so simple to jump into trading using the preset system default values that novice traders often begin trading without testing different parameters or educating themselves on the proper interpretation of an indicator because of the desire to make money quickly! As a result, the RSI is also one of the most widely misused technical indicators!

Once understood and correctly applied, the Relative Strength Index has the ability to indicate whether prices are trending, when a market is overbought or oversold, and the best price to enter or exit a trade. It can also indicate what trading timeframe is most active and provides information in determining key price levels of support and . resistance. However, in order to fully understand the Relative Strength Index, we must first understand how price behavior affects it.

The calculated value for Wilder's RSI oscillates between 0 and 100. This value represents a ratio of the average recent time period price 'gains' to the average recent time period price 'losses' calculated over a number of time periods. In other words, it compares the internal strength of a security or market. A trip into any professional trading office in the world will reveal at least one or two charts with this indicator being plotted on at least one monitor. It is the opinion of many professional traders that this one indicator, of all the widely known indicators - is the most versatile and powerful indicator that is available.

This book will attempt to convey the information that a trader would want or need to know about the Relative Strength Index. There is a considerable body of information that has been gathered concerning the RSI since 1978 when Mr. Wilder promoted this indicator in his groundbreaking book. While it is impossible to discuss all of the knowledge that is available on the subject of the RSI, when you have finished studying this short book you will know how to use it to determine:

1. The current trend.
2. The best entry/exit prices for a trade.
3. Price levels where contra-trend market retracement will likely end.
4. Basic Price Retracement Theory and Momentum Discrepancy Reversal Points.
5. What is meant by the term "timeframe".
6. How to determine the dominant market "timeframe".
7. When a different "timeframe" is negating or overpowering the present timeframe.
8. How to determine upside or downside price objectives that have high probability of being reached.

Every profitable trader has learned that he or she must possess their own "edge" that enables them to regularly extract money from the market place. For a trader to have an "edge," he or she must have an accurate perception of the market that is also *unique*. The applied definition of a trader with an "edge" is a trader with an accurate perception of the market place that differs from other trader's perceptions. The converse of this argument is that if all of the other traders have or get the same <u>perception</u> of the market, the trading "edge" will quickly disappear. Including this thought makes it natural to expect that any advantages found in using the RSI would have long since disappeared since Mr. Wilder published his original information about the indicator in 1978.

While this expectation might be true in a perfect trading world, it is not the case in the chaotic world that we live in. The advanced and largely unknown concepts mentioned in this book are as effective today in 2004, as they were in 1978 when *"<u>New Concepts</u>"* first hit the bookstands. *In fact, these advanced concepts with some modifications can also be beneficially applied to other momentum-based indicators.*

If asked, many seasoned traders will tell a novice trader that it is important to focus on truly mastering one indicator. It is essential to know when and why an indicator is about to behave in a certain way. Once an indicator is truly mastered, the trader is able to apply his own unique perceptions and rules to it. Many inexperienced traders want to believe that they have mastered an indicator simply because they know its particular trading "rules" governing entries, exits and stops. The reality is that they "know" no more than any other trading novice. Consequently, they have no "edge" versus other traders when using a particular indicator, which is one of the primary reasons that 99% of all new traders lose their money.

It is my hope that you as the reader will take some time to realize how the RSI functions and see the dramatic benefits that can be obtained by using it in a more proficient manner. Once mastered, the Relative Strength Index provides key information telling when the market is trending and when it is overbought or oversold. The RSI can also provide strategic price levels to enter or exit market positions and give insight into when it is best to stand aside. In my mind, there is no other widely known indicator that is as effective and/or profitable!

This book is divided into two sections. In Section I, the focus is on developing the basic knowledge of the Relative Strength Index that is necessary to use with the advanced concepts. Without a thorough understanding of the basic concepts that are involved, the trader will have neither the <u>courage</u> nor <u>confidence</u> to consistently take action when the price action conveys a valuable clue.

Section II focuses on integrating the basic knowledge of price behavior, retracement theory and various timeframes with RSI theory. Also in Section II, we will learn how to enter and exit trades more profitably.

CHAPTER 2

RSI MATH

It is an accepted fact that the simple geometric formula resolutely declaring, "pi (3.1416) times 'd,' the diameter of a circle" yields its circumference. This simple formula has dramatically changed the world that we live in. The formula for calculating the Relative Strength Index is also relatively simple. In some ways, this formula for calculating the Relative Strength Index has just as profoundly changed the trading world in the few short years since its introduction.

In this section, we will discuss the math and perhaps more importantly, the logic of the math that is used in computing the Relative Strength Index. The single ending RSI value is the ratio calculation between the average increase in price versus the average decrease in price over a pre-defined period of time. It is a front-weighted momentum indicator, which gives it the ability to respond quickly to price changes. Because of its mathematical construction, it is also less affected by the sharp price swings that occur from time to time in markets.

There are two equations that are involved in solving the formula. The first component equation obtains the initial Relative Strength (RS) value, which is the ratio of the average UP closes to the average DOWN closes over 'N' periods represented in the following formula:

RS = Average of 'N' day's closes UP/Average of 'N' day's closes DOWN

The actual RSI value is calculated by indexing the indicator to 100 through the use of the following formula:

$$RSI = 100 - (100 / 1 + RS)$$

$$100 - \left(\frac{100}{1 + RS} \right)$$

This second component equation yields the final RSI value. To calculate the first value of the RSI, the previous 'N' days' price data is required. From then on, all that is needed is the data from the previous day.

In calculating for the value for RSI on succeeding days, the 'sum of gain' in price in 'N' time and the 'sum of loss' in price in 'N' time is multiplied by one less than the fixed period of time 'N'. The gain or loss for the next subsequent bar is added and the resulting number is divided by the fixed period of time 'N'. We can see this in the following formula.

RSI = 100 – (100/1+[(((Sum of gain in price in 'N-1' past intervals* 'N-1')+Gain this bar) / 'N' / ((Sum of loss in price in 'N-1' past intervals* 'N-1') + Loss this bar) / 'N']

Where:

RSI_i = Initial RSI value
'N' is the length of time intervals that is referenced in the past. For example, 14 of the prior bars.

In other words, 'N' is an interval of time. If the price action that is plotted is where each day is represented by 1 bar, and if N = 5, the RSI value is looking back at the last 5 days.

Table #1 (on the following page) shows the values in calculating the RSI where N = 14 in a hypothetical market.

Table # 1 – RSI Calculation

	Close	Chg	Gain	Loss	AvgGain	AvgLoss	RS	RSI
	1161.32							
1	1161.28	0.0400	0	0.0400				
2	1161.39	0.1100	0.1100	0				
3	1160.75	-0.6400	0	0.6400				
4	1160.71	-0.0400	0	0.0400				
5	1160.79	0.0800	0.0800	0				
6	1160.16	0.6300	0	0.6300				
7	1159.67	-0.4900	0	0.4900				
8	1159.74	0.0700	0.0700	0				
9	1159.18	-0.5600	0	0.5600				
10	1158.99	-0.1900	0	0.1900				
11	1159.24	0.2500	0.2500	0				
12	1158.93	-0.3100	0	0.3100				
13	1158.94	0.0100	0.0100	0				
14	**1158.77**	**-0.1700**	**0**	**0.1700**	**0.0371**	**0.2136**	**0.1739**	**14.815**
15	1158.78	0.0100	0.0100	0	0.0352	0.1983	0.1775	15.075
16	1157.7	1.0800	0	1.0800	0.0327	0.2613	0.1251	11.120
17	1157.09	0.6100	0	0.6100	0.0304	0.2862	0.1061	9.589
18	1156.88	0.2100	0	0.2100	0.0282	0.2808	0.1004	9.123
19	1156.56	0.3200	0	0.3200	0.0262	0.2836	0.0923	8.450
20	1156.57	0.0100	0.0100	0	0.0250	0.2633	0.0950	8.677
21	1156.61	0.0400	0.0400	0	0.0261	0.2445	0.1067	9.641
22	1156.75	0.1400	0.1400	0	0.0342	0.2270	0.1507	13.100
23	1156.71	0.0400	0	0.0400	0.0318	0.2137	0.1487	12.947
24	1157.06	0.3500	0.3500	0	0.0545	0.1984	0.2747	21.552

It should be noted that it takes many more days of data to smooth the RSI value. This table is an example only. See point Number 2 in the list below.

If you would like to see the Excel spreadsheet formulas on constructing this spreadsheet, please see Appendix A.

There are a few main points to remember about the RSI calculation:
1. The second formula changes the structure of the RSI from a simple moving average of the gains and/or losses to an exponential moving average.
2. The second formula requires at least 10 times 'N' time intervals to stabilize the RSI value and it is better to have to have 20 times 'N'. In other words, if N = 14 days, then we need 140 days of prior data for the RSI value to be of use. This is assuming daily data is used.
3. The second formula, because it is an exponential moving average, incorporates all prior price behavior into the RSI value. This adds more weight to the preceding bar price behavior.
4. As 'N' or time periods used becomes larger, the RSI value oscillates less vigorously. As 'N' becomes smaller, the oscillations of the indicator become more pronounced.

On the following page is an example of how changing 'N' changes the RSI amplitude:

Table # 2 – RSI Look-back 3 periods versus 14 periods.

	Close	RSI N = 3	RSI N = 14
	1161.32		
1	1161.28		
2	1161.39		
3	1160.75	15.49	
4	1160.71	14.29	
5	1160.79	30.53	
6	1160.16	9.43	
7	1159.67	5.22	
8	1159.74	13.49	
9	1159.18	6.59	
10	1158.99	5.23	
11	1159.24	32.68	
12	1158.93	21.24	
13	1158.94	22.55	
14	1158.77	15.83	14.815
15	1158.78	17.98	15.075
16	1157.70	3.49	11.120
17	1157.09	2.07	9.589
18	1156.88	1.71	9.123
19	1156.56	1.23	8.450
20	1156.57	2.52	8.677
21	1156.61	9.64	9.641
22	1156.75	34.67	13.100
23	1156.71	30.99	12.947
24	1157.06	71.16	21.552

So, what can we tell about the RSI at this point?

1. The RSI value oscillates in a range between 0 and 100.
2. Small changes in price will cause larger changes in the RSI value.
3. Changing the look back 'N' time interval will cause the following:
    a. The RSI amplitude swings decreases, when 'N' is increased.
    b. The RSI amplitude swings increases, when 'N' is decreased.
4. The RSI includes prior price action within its value. This requires a large number of prior time intervals for the oscillator to stabilize.

Let's explore some of the internal characteristics of the Relative Strength Index. For this demonstration, we will use the first formula of the calculation also known as the 'Morris modified RSI,' which demonstrates certain internal characteristics of the indicator. Table #3 is a spreadsheet that shows the relationships between the Gain average and the Loss average as a ratio. The most important ratios in the table are in bold print for emphasis.

Table # 3 - Ratio Table

Up Avg	Dn Avg	RSI	Up Avg	Dn Avg	RSI
1	**1**	**50.00**	**1**	**1**	**50.00**
2	**1**	**66.67**	**1**	**2**	**33.33**
3	**1**	**75.00**	**1**	**3**	**25.00**
4	**1**	**80.00**	**1**	**4**	**20.00**
5	1	83.33	1	5	16.67
6	1	85.71	1	6	14.29
7	1	87.50	1	7	12.50
8	1	88.89	1	8	11.11
9	1	90.00	1	9	10.00
10	1	90.91	1	10	9.09
11	1	91.67	1	11	8.33
12	1	92.31	1	12	7.69
13	1	92.86	1	13	7.14
14	1	93.33	1	14	6.67
15	1	93.75	1	15	6.25
16	1	94.12	1	16	5.88
17	1	94.44	1	17	5.56
18	1	94.74	1	18	5.26
19	1	95.00	1	19	5.00
20	1	95.24	1	20	4.76

The RSI value calculates to 50 if the value for the Up Average is equal to the value for the Down Average (1:1 ratio). As the Up Average increases when compared to the Down Average, the RSI value steadily increases from 50 to 100. Careful examination of Table #3 reveals that the RSI value behaves logarithmically!

As the Up Average increases to infinity and the Down Average remains steady or decreases to a level that approaches zero, the rate of increase shown by the RSI slows to a crawl. Let's take a closer look at these ratios. When the ratio is 2:1, the up average is twice as much as the down average. In this case, the Relative Strength Index value is 66.67.

It is interesting to note that when the Gain versus Loss ratio changes from 1:1 to 2:1, the change in the RSI value is 16.67 points. When the ratio moves from 2:1 to 3:1, the RSI value only increases another 8.33 points. For the Relative Strength Index to hit the '80' level, a ratio of 4:1 is needed. This is an Up Average that is four times larger than the Down Average and is a condition that does not occur very often.

Looking back at Table #3 where the ratios are reversed, when the Down Average moves from 1:1 to twice the Up Average (1:2), the RSI value decreases to the same degree as a 2:1 increase. This pattern continues throughout Table 3 as the ratio decreases.

When the ratio is 20:1 and the Up Average is 20 times the Down Average, the Relative Strength Index value at this time is only 95.24. This is a market condition that almost never occurs when the look back period is 14 bars!

By carefully studying the ratio relationships in Table # 3, we can glean the following information about the Relative Strength Index:

1. When the RSI is above 50, the indicator is telling us that the average gain exceeds the average loss.
2. When the RSI is below 50, the indicator is telling us that the average loss exceeds the average gain.
3. The RSI behaves like a logarithmic curve.
4. Anytime the ratio exceeds 10:1, the market has been experiencing a very strong move up.
5. Anytime the ratio exceeds 1:10, the market has been experiencing a very strong down move.
6. The largest increase or decrease in the RSI value occurs when the ratio changes from 1:1 to the next whole number (2:1 or 1:2).
7. The RSI value experiences its largest changes in value as it oscillates between the index values of 40 and 60. In other words the RSI is most sensitive to price change when the RSI is oscillating between 40 and 60.

As we shall see later, these observations are crucial to fully understanding the interplay between price activity and the RSI. It is not enough to understand that you should take a certain action whenever the RSI does this and/or that. It is important that you also understand the "why!"

CHAPTER 3

PRICE BEHAVIOR

A thorough discussion of price behavior deserves its own book. However, in our effort to understand the Relative Strength Index, we will limit our discussion to the price behavior characteristics that relate to how the RSI behaves.

In this section, we will discuss price behavior. Unfortunately, when the majority of traders consider <u>price behavior</u>, they immediately think of <u>price patterns</u>. Price behavior causes the creation of certain bar (price) patterns that are visible on a price chart. Just as the moon creates tidal forces that create high and low tides, price behavior creates price patterns. We could plot the levels of high and/or low tide on a chart and use the information contained in the chart to surf or launch a boat. However, simply seeing the frequency of high and low tide levels will not explain what has caused the different tide levels that are shown on our chart. Similarly, a price chart displays various patterns that could be used to generate profits. But without understanding the why of how these patterns were created, we will not be able to trade as profitably as we possibly could. This chapter focuses on the 'why.' What are the forces that cause bull and bear markets? To profitably use the Relative Strength Index, we must understand certain <u>minimum concepts</u> regarding price behavior.

The price for any commodity futures contract or security is based upon the beliefs of the strongest group in the trading arena. Many people think that they understand price action – most do not. If the majority of traders really understood price action, the constant up and down volatility that we see in the market place would largely disappear. In its place, we would see relatively steady prices with sudden huge uni-directional price movements with no contra-trend or retracement moves.

13

CORN TRADERS

The best way to explain price behavior is using an example with three hypothetical corn traders (Adam, Bob and Charlie) plus all of the on and off-floor traders. The price for a bushel of corn or any other commodity or security is the price that two traders agree to at an instant in time – free of duress. After all, if one trader is holding a gun to the other trader's head, forcing him to sell the bushel of corn cheaply, it isn't a valid trade and does not represent a valid price. If the trade was "forced", the price of that "trade" is not a valid representation of what a bushel of corn is worth in the real world and is worthless information to other traders.

Traders who agree to a mutually established price provide other traders with a certain amount of information. This information may or may not be valuable to some or all of the other traders. If there is only one trade, the only thing the other traders can determine is that the price these two traders think is fair is "x". Should the two traders agree a few minutes later to make another trade, then this new information will tell all of the other traders that the price has changed up, down, or has remained the same. From the trades, the other corn traders cannot tell anything more than that the price of corn has changed. It is also not possible for them to know if the trade price was made free of force. If the trade price is made under coercion/force/threat, then that trade price is invalid. *For example, if we assume that both corn traders are well informed traders and neither one is under any pressure to buy or sell corn other than a desire to profit, then the price the corn is traded at represents a valid price. Should the trade be made because of force or coercion, the price of the trade is invalid.*

Why is this price information important? Because at its most simple level, all that is needed to make a market place are two traders who agree upon a price of exchange. Many people think that the market is constantly determining the "best" or most "accurate" price for a particular commodity or security. This typical view is that price is an accurate representation of all known information at the instant in time that a trade was made. The point that I am trying to illustrate is that price is often nothing more than a number that two traders agree to and nothing more. I realize that this is opposite of what many "experts" say.

There are many types of traders. In this example, we are using corn but in reality, these types of traders exist in all markets. Listed below are just some possible classifications:

1. Small Corn Producer – knowledgeable only about his local market place and his farm.
2. Large Corn Producer – knowledgeable about his national market place and the farming conditions in the nation.

3. Large International Diversified Corn Producer – knowledgeable about the international market place and the growing conditions internationally.
4. Small Corn Reseller – intimate knowledge about local market
5. Medium Corn Reseller – knowledgeable about national market place.
6. Large International Reseller – knowledgeable about international market place.
7. Small Speculator – limited capitalization, limited ability to withstand losing positions.
8. Medium Speculator – better capitalization with the ability to withstand losing positions while waiting for market reversals.
9. Large Institutional – Significant capitalization, lots of "brain power" with the ability to hold large positions for long periods of time regardless of price movement.
10. Large Speculator – Immense capitalization, lots of "brain power" with the ability to hold large positions for long periods of time regardless of price movement.

There are many more "types" of traders. Conventional wisdom tells us that price is an accurate representation of the corn market. So, if our two corn traders are small corn producers and they agree to a price on a small amount of produce – does their price reflect the "fair" price for corn? Do you think that a large international agricultural business concern like Archer-Daniels-Midland believes this is a "fair" price for corn?

I am not saying that the price agreement made by 2 small corn producers is not important because it is. I am saying that it is important to realize that without any knowledge of who made a trade or whether a trade was made free of force or threat, the price of a trade is nothing more than a number. This is also the number that everyone feeds into their computers for the software to crunch the numbers and display an indicator line on a computer screen.

For those of you that believe that ADM or other large international concerns do not care a hoot about these two traders, I can tell you about other traders who believe that the two local corn farmers have a more intimate knowledge of the growing conditions of corn, and consequently their "price" is more valid.

Our two corn traders could be anyone. Let's assume that the market has just opened and we have Adam offering to buy (bidding) corn at 219.00 and Bob who is offering (asking) 220.50 for his corn! They agree on 220.00, generating the first trade of the day. A minute elapses and Charlie decides to accept Bob's asking price of 220.50. Bob and Charlie, after conducting their business, are no longer interested in any more trades. The increase in price causes a few other traders in the pit to see that the price is going up so they consequently jump into the action, bidding for some corn, pushing prices to 225.00.

Adam, seeing a chance to make some easy money, decides to sell the corn contract he purchased at 220.00 and a second contract making him short the market. This trade takes place at 225.25. Upon seeing a trade at 225.25, Charlie reconsiders his position and decides that now would be a good time to add to his long position by buying 100 contracts. In his buying frenzy, he continually accepts the asking (or offering) price. Consequently, traders who desired to sell their corn contracts see an active buyer steadily raising the offering price to 230.00.

Adam realizes that he is unable to hold his short position at 225.25 because he doesn't have the capital to meet the margin requirements, decides to buy a contract to exit his short position. However, because of Charlie's rush to buy his large position, the sellers have raised their offer to 235.00 and will not accept anything lower! This _forces_ Adam to hit the ask and take a 10-cent loss! At this time an off-floor trader decides that these prices are unreasonable and decides to sell one and two contracts at a time to establish a short position just as Adam had attempted earlier. However, he has the capitalization to hold his position until prices drop and he lowers his asking price to less than 235.00, which was the asking price of all of the other corn sellers.

This off-floor trader lowers his asking price to 234.50. At this price, his offer is the best price available to the buyers in the pit. They hit his asking price and their orders are filled immediately. As our off-floor trader wants to establish a large short position, he lowers his offer below the other competing sellers again and his asking price is hit again. Our off-floor trader continues to lower his offer until he has no more desire to sell, which causes the competing sellers to lower their offers.

Every novice trader understands this simple example of price generation. What many traders do not realize is that the price activity was conveying no more important information about how healthy the current corn crop was going to be in the fall than it was forecasting the price of apples next spring. The price information was conveying the _perception_ of corn traders that corn would be more expensive in the future. The "why" it would be more expensive _was totally unimportant_.

Adam, with the first short position, and our off-floor trader both perceived that prices were too high and should reverse and move lower. Unfortunately, Adam entered his short position too early and was forced to exit his trade with a loss. The pricing decision where Adam exited his losing trade was not made free of duress. Adam had to exit this trade because he was unable to meet the anticipated margin call to maintain his position. Since this trade was made under duress, was the price high of 235.00 representative of the market internals? Did it represent the real value of corn? No, it represented the value corn sellers perceived in the instant of time they were focused upon. Whenever sellers agree that the price will continue higher and refuse to lower their offering or asking prices, you are seeing a market that has become hysterical. Just because corn traded at 235.00 while Charlie was acquiring his position was irrelevant.

CHAPTER 4

THE REAL NATURE OF THE MARKET PLACE

What is the real nature of the market place? The market place simply consists of traders that are focused on a unit of time with every expectation that the market price action will move in their favor within their established unit of time. Traders have varying levels of capitalization, experience and risk tolerance. Since traders have different levels of capitalization, they also have different time horizons or time "envelopes" that they choose to focus on. When the market behaves in a certain fashion within this "unit of time," the trader who is focusing on this "unit of time" will undertake a certain action or actions.

The reason that prices move is because of how traders perceive the reality of the market place in a certain unit of time as dictated by their capitalization, experience, and risk tolerance. " In every sense of the word, market action is a fight between traders focused on what the price will be doing in 5 minutes versus those who only care about where the market will be in 5 days, 5 weeks or 5 months. To complicate matters a little more, some of these combatants are using their rent money while others have more capitalization than the Gross National Product of many of the world's countries!

Generally, the larger the capitalization of the trader, the longer he or she is willing to wait for prices to move in their direction. As the capitalization level increases, the ability to withstand unfavorable price action increases as well. Very well capitalized traders are also unable to establish large positions at one time without moving the market price against their position. This is why they must buy on weakness and sell on strength. These well-capitalized traders generally "fade" the trend of the traders who are focused on shorter time units than they are focused on.

So, what am I saying here? The price you are seeing on your computer screen is nothing more than a number. It could be the result of two "billion dollar hedge funds" agreeing to trade 10,000 contracts at a price, or it could be two producers plowing on the 'back 40 acres' agreeing to trade a one lot at a price. You don't know. *The price is where traders of different timeframe perspectives and capitalization levels come together in an instant of time agreeing on a certain price. In order to understand where prices are going, it is important to understand which "time perspective" is the stronger force, and then go with that force.*

"The FORCE is more your friend than the trend."

Making an attempt to determine where prices are going by using only a daily chart or a 5 minute chart (or whatever timeframe you like or want to trade in) is much like standing in the trading pit trying to determine which floor traders are filling orders for the traders with better knowledge and/or capitalization. In many ways, using only one bar chart plotted in one unit of time is a losing proposition. To become a great trader, you must develop the ability to look at price charts in different time units such as monthly, weekly, daily, 60-minute, 30-minute and 5-minute bars. You need to have the ability to recognize which timeframe (or level of capitalization) is creating the price action. There are times when floor traders (as shown on a 50 second bar chart) are creating all of the volatility in the market. There are other times that it will be the 60-minute traders who are dominating the action. While at other times, it will be the weekly traders who are the dominant force in the market.

The Relative Strength Index will help identify which timeframe is in charge because it instantly conveys vast amounts of market information which is mostly ignored by other traders. I am not saying that price is not important at any one moment or that one category of trader is more informed than another group of traders. Price is extremely important and even large hedge funds can go 'belly up.' What I am trying to emphasize is that the two opposing parties of a trade are often focused on different timeframes and have totally different capitalization levels.

Conventional trading wisdom says that if Adam buys corn at 220.00 from Bob and prices decline to 219.00, Adam is upset because he is losing money. Adam might not care that the price has declined to 219.00 or 209.00 because he is focused on a much longer timeframe! Should this be the case, both traders still believe that they got a fair price and both traders are happy with their market positions.

CHAPTER 5

PRICE BEHAVIOR & THE RSI

What price behavior goes with or compliments the Relative Strength Index behavior? As we shall see, there are certain RSI behavioral characteristics that indicate certain things such as market reversals, trends, weakening of trend. In many cases, there are certain price behaviors that coincide with this RSI behavior.

When we choose a certain unit of time to create a chart, we have decided to focus our attention on those traders that also think that this timeframe is important. For example, if we are looking at a 5-minute chart, we will be focusing on other traders who also think a 5-minute chart is (or might be) important. The term "timeframe" merely refers to the time interval used in creating the bars on the chart. A trader with a 5-minute timeframe is looking at a chart where the time interval of each bar is 5 minutes. Likewise, a trader with a 30-minute timeframe constructs charts with bar intervals of 30 minutes.

Let's talk about how prices move from the perspective of traders observing the market from different timeframes. Generally, traders focus 90% of their energies on one timeframe. The other 10% of their energy is spent looking at the infinite variety of other timeframe choices that are available. A 5-minute trader might also look at a 30-minute chart, a tick chart, and a daily chart. A 60-minute trader might choose to observe a 10-minute chart and a 240-minute chart. It is important to consider that the combinations of time unit intervals are endless.

In the following example, we will use a 5, 15, 60 and 240-minute charts. Corn has been moving sideways between 210 and 230 for the last three days. Naturally, there are traders that sell corn every time the price approaches 230 and buy when it approaches 210. In our example, today the price goes to 230 and then continues higher to 230.50 making a new 3-day high. This new high is very clearly seen by 5-minute traders using a 5-minute chart.

As prices climb above 230 on a 5, 15, 60 and 240-minute chart, in the first 5 minutes of trading the current bar is going up. If we were looking at a Japanese Candlestick chart, the candles would be all white in all timeframes. After the first 5 minutes above 230, the price continues to climb to 232. On the 5-minute chart, there are 2 bars going up. On the 15, 60, and 240-minute charts, we still have only one bar moving higher. If the price over the next 3 hours rallies to 240, we will see 36 bars on the 5-minute chart reflecting this climb higher. We will see 12 bars on the 15-minute chart, 3 bars on the 60-minute chart, and only the current bar in the 240-minute chart.

Seldom will you see all of the bars in all of the charts moving in the same direction. Usually, you will see a rally followed by a retracement followed by a new rally to new highs. Because of the different time perspectives of different traders, the different charts show the struggle between the Bears and Bulls who are focused on their own timeframes.

When the price originally moved above 230, it might have caught the attention of everyone in all timeframes or only the attention of the short-term 5-minute traders. Typically, the longer timeframe traders don't care too much if the price moves above a previous high on a shorter timeframe chart by one or two ticks. They want to see a larger breakout or see how prices behave after the breakout. In any case, as the price moved above 230, the short timeframe traders noticed the breakout and began to actively bid for corn with the more anxious ones hitting the asking/offer price. As more and more traders hit the offer and the number of buyers increased, the traded price of corn is also pushed higher.

This is a key point to understand – there is a limit to how <u>long</u> the short-term traders will perceive that the current price is "cheap." As soon as the 5-minute traders perceive that the last trade is no longer "cheap," the 5-minute traders will <u>all</u> stop actively bidding for corn. It is at this point that the buyers are no longer willing to buy at the offer/ask price. This reality causes one or more sellers to accept something lower than the offer and prices will begin to drop. The only thing that will save the 5-minute Bulls is if the traders in the <u>next</u> longer timeframe believe that prices could be ready to rally and begin to buy. For example, the 5-minute traders began to buy because prices had rallied to a point where they had "broken through resistance" and were moving higher. For the next longer timeframe traders to also think that prices are moving higher, the 5-minute traders must push prices high enough to convince them from their timeframe perspective.

If the Bulls in the next longer timeframe, for instance 15-minute traders, decide to buy because of a breakout, then the 5-minute Bulls are saved while the 5-minute Bears are losing money. These 5-minute Bears are now forced to cover their short positions as prices continue to rally. This rippling process continues as long as the traders in each next longer timeframe perspective enter the market in the same direction.

A short-term rally will fizzle if the shorter-term traders push prices higher and the next longer timeframe traders decide that prices are "too high." These traders can begin to short or fade the rally or do nothing, waiting to buy the retracement. Because the longer timeframe traders are typically better capitalized and can trade more contracts, they have the ability to stop this upward price movement. If the longer timeframe traders begin to earnestly sell into the rally, they will hit the bid causing the offers to decline and immediately halt the increasing price of corn. This activity is best revealed in the primary as well as the shorter timeframe charts of the sellers.

Once these longer-term timeframe traders begin to short the rally, they have in effect drawn a line in the sand. They have told ALL of the shorter timeframe traders what price they believe is "too high." At this point, the battle of whose perception of the corn market is correct has commenced. Do the shorter-term traders have the correct perception that prices are ultimately going higher or do the longer timeframe traders have it right?

When the retracement of a rally is shallow, it indicates a stronger opinion of the shorter timeframe traders versus the opinion of the longer-term traders. Alternatively, if the longer timeframe traders agree with the shorter timeframe traders (that the market is ultimately heading higher), they stand aside rather than fading the previous rally knowing that the 5-minute Bulls will exhaust themselves and prices will retrace. This is when they look to enter the market. If the price of corn retraces less than 33% of the prior rally, then we could say that the 5-minute Bulls are stronger and/or the 15-minute traders agree with the shorter-term timeframe opinion. Should the Bears push the retracement to 50% or more, the 5-minute traders are probably being overpowered by a more powerful longer timeframe. Should the retracement be more than 66%, the traders in the shorter timeframe that caused the price movement would be in trouble.

In the next section, we cover Retracement in more depth. The point for now is that it is the shorter timeframe traders that created the initial rally and it is the longer timeframe traders that halt it, or fail to push prices higher. These short-term traders will only bid the price higher to a point. It is at this point that the professional short-term traders begin to take their profits. The only thing that can save the novice short-term traders is the traders in the next longer timeframe (15 minute in this example) deciding that prices have potential to move higher causing them to bid the price higher.

It is just as likely that prices will be pushed lower as the longer term traders decide that prices are too high and begin selling. After halting the rally by selling into its strength and forcing prices lower, the longer term traders may decide that prices are low enough to begin buying, eventually pushing prices to new highs. This is usually done after pushing prices below the previous lows and panicking the shorter-term traders allowing the longer-term traders to once again fade the shorter-term traders by buying into weakness. As these different timeframe traders struggle over whose perception is more correct, the retracements and rallies reveal themselves in the bar charts and more importantly in the RSI. The Relative Strength Index reveals when the next longer timeframe traders agree with the shorter timeframe traders and when they disagree.

If everyone agrees that prices are moving higher, market prices will move up strongly. On the days when there is the strongest agreement, there is a limit move! On these days, prices move in only one direction and pity the poor trader who happens to be opposite this move!

Because there are so many different markets and different timeframes in these markets, it becomes extremely difficult to describe a universal sequence of bars that will indicate when the shorter-term traders are tired. Each market and timeframe is different and has a different look. This is a subject that is very complex and is well beyond the goals of this book

As a trader, you are looking for a certain pattern, behavior of price, or indicator that re-occurs in what appears to be random fashion. When this pattern does occur, it signals a reversal in price. This pattern may not occur at every price reversal but it usually indicates a reversal with a high degree of probability. For example, when looking at a 5-minute chart of the cash S&P 500, a price pattern that occurs occasionally just before prices reverse lower is 2 bullish belt hold lines with the close being at the high appearing within a rally. A quick explanation of bullish belt hold lines is that it is a candlestick formation where the open is also the low and the close is at or very near the high.

The 2 bullish belt hold lines work whenever the 5-minute timeframe traders are dominant. When a longer timeframe enters the battle, this pattern fails. The longer timeframe could be 7, 10, 15, 18 minutes or whatever. This logic works today (2/2002), but probably will not work in the future because the market characteristics are constantly changing. As a result, the candlestick characteristic will need to be changed or the number of belt hold lines referenced in the past might need to be changed.

You are the one to best determine what price behavior will indicate to you when a particular timeframe is dominant. I realize that this task may appear daunting, but it is not as difficult as it initially appears. You want to discover a bar or candlestick relationship that occurs at market tops or bottoms. It is okay if this behavior doesn't work all of the time because the failure will indicate that a different timeframe has become the dominant player. How do you know when a particular timeframe is dominant in a market rally or decline? When the price advances or declines and the pattern looks like a staircase, it usually indicates one timeframe being dominant.

Build a chart using Japanese Candlesticks in whatever timeframe you prefer, print 30 pages of charts, identify the tops and bottoms, and begin looking for candlestick patterns. Look at the relationships of the shadows, opens, highs, lows, and closes. Keep in mind that you are looking for relationships that occur infrequently. When they do occur, they typically indicate a top or bottom. It is not important if they fail at times, you are using these patterns in conjunction with analyzing the RSI. The RSI is the primary vehicle that we are going to trade with. You will use these relationships as an aid to identify tops and bottoms.

Chapter 6

Basic Retracement Theory

In the previous chapter, we learned that the capitalization level of a trader largely determines the timeframe that they focus the greatest amount of energy upon. In our analysis, we want to know what timeframe is in control or has the momentum and align our trading with that timeframe. As traders, we want to trade with the group that most closely matches our own capitalization and time horizons. However, we must always trade in alignment with the strongest momentum. There are three ways to accomplish this: a thorough understanding of price movement, retracement levels, and the Relative Strength Index.

A common question concerning timeframe is, "What is considered a long or short timeframe?" This determination is subjective to each trader and is largely based upon his or her capitalization. The "timeframe" generally preferred is the average price range within a fixed interval of time translated into money falling within the risk tolerance of the trader. In other words, an undercapitalized trader that has difficulty meeting the margin requirement for the S&P E-Mini may be comfortable with a $200 loss, which corresponds to the average range of a 5-minute bar – but would be devastated with a $2,000 loss, which corresponds to the range of a two-hour or four-hour bar. As a result, an undercapitalized trader will focus most of his energy on trading a 5-minute chart. The better-capitalized trader will focus most of his energy on trading a longer timeframe such as the 2-hour bars.

From this point forward, I will use the S&P for the duration of the book. When day trading, there are three dominant timeframes that have a crucial influence: the big timeframe (daily chart), the intermediate timeframe (30-minute chart), and the short-term timeframe (5-minute chart). Generally, this is true for all markets. In the following examples, I will be using a 5-minute chart. Please note that the percentages apply in all markets and timeframes. When position trading, the three dominant timeframes are daily, weekly and monthly.

To fully explain the theory of retracement would require another book because it is a very involved subject. However, the following explanations of <u>basic retracement concepts</u> should suffice in understanding the RSI.

Before discussing retracement theory, we need to discuss a mathematician named Leonardo Fibonacci de Pisa, who lived in the year 1202 A.D. He decided to investigate how fast rabbits could breed under ideal hypothetical circumstances. He wanted to determine how many pairs of rabbits he would have if he placed one breeding pair of 2 week-old rabbits in a field. Female rabbits conceive at one month of age with a gestation period of one month. At the end of two months, the female can bear babies. For this problem, Fibonacci limited the number of hypothetical babies a female could bear at two (one female, one male). He further assumed that the rabbits would never die and every female would produce two rabbits every month from the second month forward for the next year.

At the end of Month # 1, the two rabbits mate and there is 1 pair of rabbits. At the end of Month # 2, there is the initial pair and a new pair of baby rabbits, giving 2 pairs of rabbits. At the end of Month # 3, the initial pair has another set of babies, giving 3 pairs of rabbits. At the end of Month # 4, another pair of baby rabbits is born to the initial pair and a pair of baby rabbits born to the first pair of babies born at the end of the second month giving us 5 pairs of rabbits. By continuing this exercise, you can see that the sequence is: 1, 1, 2, 3, 5, 8, 13, 21, 34, ... The formula is for the sequence is:

$$f(n)=f(n-1)+f(n-2), \text{ if } n>2.$$

This sequence of numbers (1, 1, 2, 3, 5, 8, 13, 21, 34, ..) is seen in nature when one examines the family tree of honeybees. The family tree of a male drone bee has the following: one parent (male drone bees result from the queen's unfertilized eggs), 2 grand parents, 3 great grand parents, 5 great-great-grand-parents, and 7 great-great-great-grand-parents. This cycle also occurs in other natural phenomenon.

We can see that the Fibonacci number sequence occurs in nature by counting the number of petals on a flower. Some flowers have a very precise number of petals, while others, if averaged, will have the following number of petals.
http://www.mcs.surrey.ac.uk/Personal/R.Knott/Fibonacci/shell.gif

Table # 4 – Fibonacci Numbers in Flowers

# Petals	Flower
3	Lily, Iris
5	Buttercup, Wild Rose, Larkspur, Columbine
8	Delphiniums
13	Ragwort, Cineraria
21	Aster, Chicory
34	Plantain, pyrethrum
55, 89	Michaelmas daisies

Table # 5 – The First 50 Fibonacci Numbers (numbers in BOLD are also prime numbers)

0	55	6,765	832,040
1	**89**	10,946	1,346,269
1	144	17,711	2,178,309
2	**233**	**28,657**	3,524,578
3	377	46,368	5,702,887
5	610	75,025	9,227,465
8	987	121,393	14,930,352
13	**1,597**	196,418	24,157,817
21	2,584	317,811	39,088,169
34	4,181	**514,229**	63,245,986

Does anyone remember where the Dow Jones Industrial Average encountered resistance in 1973 or 2000?

If we place the Fibonacci number sequence in a column and divide the first Fibonacci number by the next successive Fibonacci number, we obtain the series of numbers in Column A. If we divide each number by the one preceding it, we find the following series of numbers in Column B.

Table #6 – Fibonacci Ratio Products

Fibonacci #	A Row #N / Row N + 1	B Row #N / Row N - 1
1		
1	1.00000	1.00000
2	0.50000	2.00000
3	0.66667	1.50000
5	0.60000	1.66667
8	0.62500	1.60000
13	0.61538	1.62500
21	0.61905	1.61538
34	0.61765	1.61905
55	0.61818	1.61765
89	0.61798	1.61818
144	0.61806	1.61798
233	0.61803	1.61806
377	0.61804	1.61803
610	0.61803	1.61804

We can expand on the concept of dividing a Fibonacci number by a subsequent Fibonacci number and get the following table (where "N" is the Row #):

Table # 7 – Fibonacci subsequent ratios

Fibonacci #	N/N+1	N/N+2	N/N+3	N/N+4	N/N+5	N/N+6
1						
1	**1.0000**	0.5000	0.3333	0.2000	0.1250	0.0769
2	**0.5000**	**0.3333**	0.2000	0.1250	0.0769	0.0476
3	**0.6667**	0.4000	0.2500	0.1538	0.0952	0.0588
5	0.6000	0.3750	0.2308	0.1429	0.0882	0.0545
8	0.6250	0.3846	0.2381	0.1471	0.0909	0.0562
13	0.6154	0.3810	0.2353	0.1455	0.0899	0.0556
21	0.6190	0.3824	0.2364	0.1461	0.0903	0.0558
34	0.6176	0.3818	0.2360	0.1458	0.0901	0.0557
55	0.6182	0.3820	0.2361	0.1459	0.0902	0.0557
89	0.6180	0.3819	0.2361	0.1459	0.0902	0.0557
144	0.6181	0.3820	0.2361	0.1459	0.0902	0.0557
233	0.6180	0.3820	0.2361	0.1459	0.0902	0.0557
377	**0.6180**	**0.3820**	**0.2361**	**0.1459**	**0.0902**	**0.0557**

These ratios quickly approach equilibrium where the result barely changes. We can take these numbers and create a table of retracement levels that are based upon the Fibonacci number sequence. This is the Retracement Table.

Table # 8 – Fibonacci Retracements Table

0.0557
0.0902
0.1459
0.2361
0.3333
0.3820
0.5000
0.6180
0.6667
0.7630
0.8541
0.9098
0.9443

To summarize, the Fibonacci sequence of numbers were discovered more than 800 years ago. The relationships are based on naturally occurring phenomenon that appears in fixed sequence. The primary way traders use the series is not the number sequence itself, but the ratios that are created when the numbers are divided into a preceding Fibonacci number. The decimal products of these numbers are used in retracement theory. Using retracement theory, we can enter into a new position or add to an existing position. Once prices bounce, we can use the "bounced price" as a stop price.

BASIC RETRACEMENT THEORY

When looking at a price chart, it is readily apparent that prices fluctuate up and down. These fluctuations seem to occur at random. As you become more comfortable working with the concept that there are multiple timeframes being reflected in any chart, this apparent randomness becomes more understandable. However, it is important that you understand when price retraces its prior move and finds support or resistance at 14.6%, 23.7%, 38.2%, 50%, 61.8%, 76.3%, or 85.4%, the market is telling you that it has "discovered" a key number. This is a key number that you should remember when placing your trailing stop.

If the market is rallying, we can expect that at some point the Bulls will get tired and prices will retrace a part of their preceding rally. This retracement will be more than 5.5% and less than 38.2% of the move, if the trend is strongly up. If the trend is moderately strong, the retracement will be 38.2% to 50%. The retracement will be between 50.0% and 66.7% if the trend higher is in danger of failing. If the retracement falls between 66.7% and 85.4%, the trend has a high probability of failing.

For our purposes, there are three types of basic retracement — shallow, medium, and deep. Understanding basic retracement theory will help us to identify whether a trend is strong, moderate or weak by the percentage of its retracement. In addition to basic market retracement, there are complicated retracements that involve multiple timeframes consisting of longer or shorter time cycles. These complicated retracements will not be discussed in this book. Before using retracement theory, we must allow the price to move a certain amount of points and time. For example, if we are following a rally in the S&P and are looking at a 30-minute chart, then we want the rally to move more points and last longer than on a 5-minute chart before attempting to use retracement theory.

The question that arises most often is what amount of price movement is required before retracement theory can be used effectively? To some degree, the answer is subjective. Prices retrace lower after rallying because traders in the timeframe that started the rally are tired and have overextended themselves in the rush/push to higher prices. We want to determine what amount of price movement for each dominant timeframe (day, 30 min., 5 min.) would indicate that these respective timeframes are overextended. We are looking only at price movement in the amount of points – not price patterns. There are two ways to accomplish this objective.

First Method: Determine the average price movement for the average rally/ decline in the timeframe that we are looking at. This is accomplished by examining at least the previous 100 or so rallies, and plunges in the timeframe to be studied. By observing the number of points before a retracement occurs on average, we can accurately judge when a move is probably over and ready to begin a retracement. For example, if we observe that for the previous 100 rallies prices in a 5-minute chart moved an average of 7 points – then we know that after market prices have moved 6 points, the professional 5-minute traders will usually be looking to take profits.

Second Method: Calculate the average price range for each bar in a longer time interval and use a percentage of that range to indicate what amount of price movement is needed before using retracement theory. The longer timeframe to use is one where "one time interval" in the longer timeframe consists of 13 shorter time intervals.

Imagine looking at a 30-minute chart of the cash S&P. We know that there are 390 minutes in the average trading day or 13 30-minute bars. In order to use retracement theory on a 30-minute chart, we need to know when the 30-minute traders are probably tired. We can examine many significant prior rallies on the 30-minute chart or we can take an average range of the high and low in the next significant longer timeframe multiplied by a factor of 13. In this case, it would be a daily timeframe as it takes 13 bars in the 30-minute chart to create 1 bar in the daily chart.

Using the 10-day average range of the S&P to indicate when the 30-minute traders are tired will tell us when we should begin to expect a market retracement. If we are using a 5-minute chart, we can use a 65-minute chart to calculate the 10 bar average range. It is important to use the average range of bars where each bar consists of the total number of smaller bars. If you were to use an average range where some of the bars consisted of less time, then the average would be in error. There are 6 hours and 30 minutes in each S&P day session. If we are using 60-minute bars to determine the 10 bar average, we must not use the last bar in the trading day in the calculation to determine the average range as it only consists of 30 minutes. It is important to know in advance how much any rally or decline must move before you consider using retracement levels.

If you are monitoring the average range of a longer timeframe in real time and it begins to compress, then a shallow retracement will probably be insignificant. Typically, the average range of a longer timeframe will not decrease. Knowing this, we can use the retracement level as a good indication of trend strength. If the market finds support with a shallow retracement (less than 38.2%) then prices should easily take out the previous high or low (if a bear market). When the retracement is deep (50% to 61.8%), it is an indication that the market is weak or weakening, and that the trend could be ending. Prices will find it difficult to take out the previous high if the market is rallying or low if the market is declining. Retracements of .618 to .854 show signs of extreme market weakness and should be viewed as an indication that the trend is probably reversing. A deep retracement also tells us that a longer timeframe has noticed the previous price movement and it was the longer timeframe traders who faded the move.

Before the trading day begins, it is important to examine the daily chart to be aware of key numbers that the longer-term traders are watching. Here are items to examine on the longer-term or daily chart:

Daily Chart Exam for determining major trend.
1. What are the major support and resistance numbers using prior rallies and declines?

2. Was there a reversing rally or decline? What was the major resistance/support level?
3. What would be the price for a 38%, 50% or 66% retracement from the most recent rally high or decline low?
4. What is the 10-day average daily range?

30 Minute Chart Exam for determining the intermediate trend:

1. Is the market making higher highs and higher lows indicating an up-trend?
2. Is the market making lower lows and lower highs indicating a downtrend?
3. Is there an up or down move that approaches 100% of the 10-day average daily range?
    a. If true, the 30-minute timeframe traders are probably exhausted or over-extended.
    b. If the move is less than 100% of the daily average range, then we will focus our attention on the next smaller timeframe.

5-Minute Chart Exam for determining the short-term trend.

1. Has the price moved 40% of the 10-day average daily range?
    a. If true, we know the 5-minute traders are probably tired.
    b. Should the 5-minute chart be indicating an entry, we will drop to a 1-minute price behavior for our trigger.

Basic retracement theory is only applied when the market is trending up or down. If the market is choppily trading sideways, we should not use retracement theory. If price has moved 40% of the 10-day average range on a 5-minute chart, we can expect that the shorter timeframe traders are tired and that a shallow retracement is imminent. Should the retracement not be shallow, it is because the longer timeframe traders decided to fade the rally. In a 5-minute chart, a rally of more than 50% of the 10-day average range is a huge move and is usually indicating that a stronger trend will develop. However, a 50% move of the 10-day range in a 30-minute chart is only a moderate move.

Assuming that we have a solid uptrend that exceeds 50% of the 10-day daily average range on a longer timeframe (30-minute or daily) chart and see a retracement of less than 38% on the shorter timeframe 5-minute chart, then we must only trade in the direction of the intermediate trend.

Table # 9 – Trend Strength as Indicated by Percentage of Retracement:

Trend Strength	Maximum Retracements	Upside Targets (downside targets are inverse)	Comments:
Very Strong	14.6% to 23.7%	A to B added to C	Easily exceed B
Strong	38.2%	A to B added to C	Easily exceed B
Medium Strong	38.2% to 50%	80% of A to B added to C	Should Easily exceed B
Medium	50%	80% of A to B added to C	Should Easily exceed B
Medium Weak	61.8% to 50%	80% of A to B added to C	Possibly exceed B
Weak	61.8%	80% of A to B added to C	Possibly exceed B
Very Weak	85.4% to 76.3%	80% of A to B added to C	Probably will not exceed B

Chart # 1 - Basic Retracement Theory - using a 30 minute chart of cash S&P

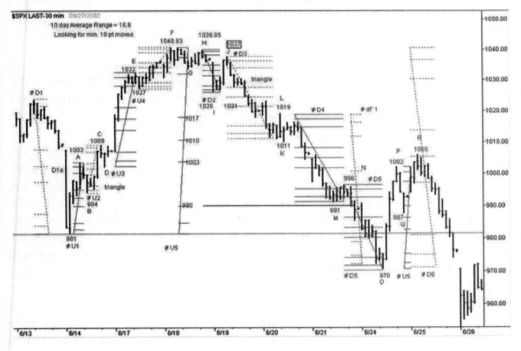

Chart # 1 – Description on the following page.

1.   In retracement D1, prices collapsed from 1023 to 981. Then, prices rallied to D1a, which is a 50% retracement. We know that the strength of the bear market is only moderate from this retracement. We know that the high at point A should not be violated if the Bears are in charge.

2.   At this point, we don't know who or what timeframe is in charge. We will draw another up retracement U1. We know that if the Bulls buy at a 38% retracement, then they are probably in charge. This is exactly what happens at 994 at point B. We can take the difference between 1003 and 981 to get an upside target of 22 points which is added to 994 giving us an upside target of 1016.

3.   As prices rally to C at 1009, the Bulls encounter resistance. This coincides with the 61.8% retracement of D1 and a downside breakaway gap. Upon seeing the down close, we could draw another retracement U2 and we see that the Bulls defended the 31% and 50% level. The rally from point B to point C is very small and we shouldn't use it on this 30-minute chart.

4.   The ensuing rally to point E totally negated the downtrend, D1, before encountering resistance at 1032. Once again in drawing our retracement levels, we can see that the Bulls prevented any retracement under 1027 (14.6%) telling us that the trend is very strong.

5.   The rally from 1027 to 1040 is labored. We draw another retracement U4. The price behavior is different than previous tops at points A and C and to some degree point E. Notice the lack of upper shadows at F. Looking at retracements, we can see that at point G, the Bears were able to close under the 38% level and just above the 50% as the Bulls seemed to be on vacation. The trend has significantly weakened from "Very Strong" to "Medium." It is not "Medium Strong" because of the down close near the 50% retracement with an intra-bar low under 50%. At this point, should the Bulls fail to protect and prevent any price extension to the downside below point G, the rally would probably be over. Additionally, point G is important as an important swing point – notice the 2 higher lows on either side of it.

6.   The Bulls managed to rally prices to 1039.85 at point H. Prices made a new intra-bar high at 1039.85 and failed to close above its open. At this point, we knew that the rally was probably over. When the Bears were able to close the market below point G and making a breakaway gap lower, the Bears were the dominant force. If we were trading in a smaller timeframe, we should have been short. However, in the 30-minute timeframe it is not apparent that the market had shifted. We must wait to see how the price behavior unfolds. Draw another retracement, U5, from the 981 low to the 1040 high. From this retracement, we can identify important support within the context of a longer timeframe.

7.   As prices fall below point G, we begin drawing our new lower retracement D2. When prices establish a new low at 1026, we knew that the Bulls would be gunning for the breakaway gap and should they fail to close above that level, the market would collapse once again. We know this because there were no other significant retracement levels nearby. The nearest long term support on U5 was 1017. This indicates that the low of 1026 was only a temporary low.

8.   As the Bulls rushed to close the breakaway gap in the 1036 area, the market closed above the 61% retracement level. The last significant resistance area for the Bulls was at 85%, which the Bulls were unable to hit. From this information, we know that the Bears will probably hit the 1017 target and possibly 1010.

9.   When prices fell under point I at 1026, it was possible that we were at the beginning of a major bear market if the Bulls failed to defend support at 1017 (38% buy retracement), or 1010 (50%). Prices continued to fall finding temporary support at 1017 and finally coming to a halt at 1011. Drawing our new retracement D3, we can see that our 38% sell retracement would be at 1021. On the next bar, the Bulls rally prices to 1019 before closing just off of the intra-bar low. For the next 3 bars, the Bulls are unable to close above the 14.6% sell retracement level. At this point, we know that the spike to 1019 was nothing more than a bull rally in a smaller timeframe than 30 minutes. We know that the bear trend is "very strong" with no close above the 14.6% retracement. In addition, we know that the bear market would become major as 1010 level was the 50% retracement of the previous rally. If the Bulls were going to buy, NOW was the time. The fact that they abandoned ship was all too obvious by the large black candle that closed under 1011. When prices closed under 1011, we knew that the Bears were dominant and would push prices towards a target of 993 as calculated by [1019-(1037-1011)]. This price was close enough to the 61% retracement level of the previous bull rally that it confirmed that prices would hit 990 before finding any support.

10.   Prices hit a low of 991 at point M. Then, they stayed in the 14.6% retracement level before selling off once again. The close above the 14.6% retracement line is ignored because it is so close to that level. We can once again project the new low to 968 from [996-(1019-991)]. Price once again hits the target. The low at point M (991) was significant as many traders began thinking that perhaps a double bottom was form- ing. However by using basic retracement theory, we could tell that the bear market trend was still "very strong." Why would anyone even think about buying it?

11.   Prices broke through major support at 981 stopping out all of the long traders who thought a double bottom was forming and found support at 970. This is where we forecast the low using retracement theory. The next bar saw the Bulls buying the market pushing prices back above 981 retracing 50% of the prior plunge in one bar. At

this point, we would draw our retracement levels, D5, and because it could also be a significant low we would draw a retracement level D6. Prices rallied to 1002 after they rallied above 986, which was the 61.8% retracement for D5. At this time, we knew that the Bear trend had changed from "very strong down" to "weak." Here we begin to focus our attention on retracement level D6.

12.   Prices rallied to point P at 1002 before encountering resistance. This price was just above the 31.8% retracement level of D6 and the 61.8% level. From our analysis, we know there is a very good possibility that the Bears in the longer timeframe than 30-minutes were once again going short - just as the Bulls should have defended 1017, 1010, and 1003. Look at the chart and compare the price action at points P and R versus point K. In any case, once we see the down close we draw up retracement level U5. In the next bar, prices collapse to point Q at 987 where we find Bulls that push prices higher as indicated by the 'hammer' formation. The 50% re-test level of U5 was 986. We can determine the upside target of 1002 from [1002-987)+987].

13.   Prices rallied to point R at 1005, which was the 50% re-test level of the major decline D6. It is at this point that the Bears must prevent the Bulls from pushing prices higher and should start hitting the bid in their rush to get short.

Chart # 2 - Basic Retracement Theory - using a 3-minute chart of S&P futures

ES U2 LAST-3 min 08/26/2002 C=974.75 -47.00 -4.60% O=975.00 H=979.75 L=945.50 V=60005400

Chart # 2 – Description:

1.   At point A, we can see that the high is 1000 just before making a triangle, which isn't visible on the 30 minute chart. The price action falls out of congestion to make a new low. This move from 1000 to 979 shows up in a 30-minute chart just as obviously as on a 3-minute chart. With the low price of 979, we can know that many sell orders were resting just under 980 and that the floor traders were gunning for them. What happens next in a small/short timeframe will tell us what to do.

2.   The Bulls rally prices to point C, which is a 61.8% retracement from point A to point B. We know that the Bear trend is "medium weak" to "weak." The indecision comes from the high wave line made at C. This is normally an indication that a top is in, which would make the Bear market "weak" instead of "medium weak." Do we buy, sell, or wait? I would wait to see what happens next as the 61.8% retracement occurs within 3 bars. If the Bulls find support at or above the 31.8% re-test level, we buy.

Otherwise, we short the market on the next rally. Prices find support at point D at 987.75. 31.8% support is at 987.25. An order to buy at 988.25 or better could have been entered because of the low from 2 bars previous. However, the safer bet would have been to wait or use a smaller timeframe for analysis. We can calculate the upside target at 1001 from [(992.25 - 979.0) + 987.75].

3.   Prices run up to 995.5 at point E making a double top in a 1-minute chart where they encounter resistance. Prices correct down to 990.75 at point F where we enter into a long trade. A buy order should have been placed at 991.5, which was a 50% retracement of point D to point E and a double bottom in a smaller timeframe. Our stop would have been just under the 61.8% retracement level at 990.5. At point F, we know that the point A to point B Bear plunge is probably over as prices have retraced more than 61.8%. This makes the Bear trend in the longer timeframe "weak." We know that the current bull rally is "strong" as measured by point B to point E. We also know that the swing point at point E is significant because there are 2 lower highs on either side of point E. We also know that with the Bulls closing prices at 995.5, they negated a minor swing point the Bears had made earlier at 994.5. Therefore, we are able to rest easy in placing our limit order at 991.5. We can predict that the upside rally should take prices to 1007.25 based on [(995.5-979.0)+990.75]

4.   Prices rally to point G at 997.5 before encountering more resistance. Once again, we draw retracement levels and see that the Bears are unable to push prices lower than the 31.8% re-test level, so we know that the up trend is still strong.

5.   When the market spikes to point H, we know that the Bulls are in trouble. We know this for several reasons. First and most important is that prices consolidate at point G for 5 bars before breaking out of the consolidation pattern. If the Bulls are firmly in charge, as basic retracement theory tells us, the market should close the bar near the high. Second, we can see that at point A the high was 1000; we have a double top and should encounter resistance there. Third, the reason the floor didn't push it higher was because there were probably a lot of buy orders and the floor would become net short. If the floor thought that prices would ultimately trade above 1000, why would they want to generate a lot of buy orders making them short? It would be better for them to establish major long positions and trigger the buy orders, allowing them to either estab-lish shorts or go flat. In any case, with the close at point H or 995.5, we must sit tight and see what the next bar tells us.

6.   The next bar is black with the closing price under the open and below the close of point H. It is at this point that we have to decide whether to take profits or move our stop order up to breakeven? The safer course of action in this case is to take our profits and look for another opportunity. If so, our trade made 5.50 points.

7.   As the rally to point H created a new high, we must re-draw our retracement levels from point F to point H. We can see that the 50% retracement level is within the lower part of the consolidation pattern. If the floor wants to panic the novice traders and make them sell, they will have to take out these lows. We know that for the up trend to remain intact the retracement should not exceed 61.8%, which corresponds to 994. If we did exit our position or if we want to add to our long position, we should place our limit order to buy at 994. The question is, "Where do we place our stop?" Generally, I like a 1-point stop, but where is support? We know that point C was at 992.25. As long as the Bulls keep prices above 991.5, which is 38.2% of point B to point H, the longer term up trend remains "very strong." I would place the stop order at 993 because everything else is too far away.

8.   After making a low at 993.5 at Point I, we can re-calculate the upside target to 1014 from [(999.5-979.0)+993.5]. Prices rally to point J making a high at 1005 before encountering resistance. Do you remember the upside target levels? We have targets at 1001, 1007.25, and 1014. As prices rallied up through 1001, we would move our stop to 996.25, which is the 61.8% re-test level. If prices hit our upside target of 1007.25, we would have taken our profits. However, that was not the case as 1005.0 at point J was the high. We can tell that prices hit resistance. The question is "Where do we exit our trade?" We know that the 38.2% re-test level on the point I to point J move is 1000.5. Since big money is made by hanging tough with a winning position, we cannot exit until there is proof that the trend strength has changed. After making the high at point J and closing down for the bar, which itself is a bad sign. Prices sell off for a second day. The low of this second bar becomes the low of the third day making a double bottom in a smaller timeframe. The close of the third day is near the daily high. It is here that we can clearly identify support on the three-minute chart - the lows of the last two bars. We are able to move our stop order to just under these lows at 1002.25. We would exit the trade with a stop order at 1002, giving us an 8-point profit, if the Bulls fail to defend 1002.25.

In summarizing basic retracement theory, the level of the retracement is a strong indication of the trend strength. Retracement theory categorizes the psychological strength of the Bulls versus the Bears using Fibonacci ratios. For example, a retracement that is less than 38.2% is a strong indication of strong bullish beliefs. Before we can use retracement theory, we must have a valid move higher or lower. The easiest way is to measure or determine a valid move is to use the average range in a timeframe that is 13 times longer than the timeframe we are using. We can use this average range or some fixed percentage of that range, to tell us when the shorter-term traders are probably getting tired and prices should retrace. Put another way, we can only apply retracement theory after prices have moved enough where the traders in the smaller timeframes are probably tired. Once prices have either rallied or declined to where these shorter timeframe traders are overextended, we can apply basic retracement theory. This helps us determine price levels that we can use to enter or add to our positions and levels where we might want to exit our positions. We are using the contra-trend to tell us what we should do. We will use these retracement levels as key numbers for our stop placements. A thorough understanding of basic retracement theory will help us tremendously in using Momentum Discrepancy Reversal Points.

CHAPTER 7

SUMMARY OF SECTION I

The primary concepts from this section are:

1. Prices reflect the perceptions of all traders who are actively buying and/or selling.
2. The current price might reflect reality or it could reflect a mass delusion.
3. There is no way to tell from the price what type of trader is <u>bidding</u> to buy or <u>offering</u> to sell.
4. Sometimes the small producer has a better feel for the price of corn than a large institution – sometimes not.
5. The market consists of marginally capitalized to very well capitalized traders.
6. The better a trader is capitalized the more contracts they <u>must</u> trade in order to obtain an adequate return on their investment.
7. Because larger capitalized traders <u>must</u> trade more contracts, they are forced to look at the "big" picture, i.e., a longer timeframe.
8. In order for the large institutions to avoid a lot of slippage, they must adopt trading strategies that <u>fade</u> the current move.
9. The real battle in the market place is between traders of different beliefs and time perspectives.
10. The one universal difference in beliefs is over what timeframe is the most advantageous to trade in. However, the larger the capitalization the longer this timeframe must be.
11. The largest struggle is which timeframe has the most accurate information concerning future events.
12. There is no "reality" of the market place – prices can and will behave in the most unexpected manner.

13. Price itself is nothing more than a number with the only semblance to reality being that one buyer and seller have agreed upon a price in an instant of time. One or both of these traders might have been under duress in making the transaction.

14. In order to trade effectively, we must identify not only which force (Bulls or Bears) are stronger, but also what timeframe is the dominant timeframe. If this dominant timeframe requires more capitalization than we have, we must have an alternative trading strategy that will enable us to enter the trade or stand aside.

15. One of the best "off the shelf" indicators that reveals the dominant timeframe is the Relative Strength Index.

16. By examining the price action in whatever timeframe you prefer, you can see that there are certain *price patterns* (not bar patterns like triangles, pennants, etc) that repeat semi-randomly and only occasionally fail.

17. As we shall see, when we combine these price patterns with an understanding of retracement theory and RSI analysis, we can have a high probability of creating trading profits.

18. Fibonacci numbers, when divided into preceding Fibonacci numbers, will generate decimal products (or ratios) that quickly approach equilibrium. These ratios are used in retracement theory.

19. Retracement Theory tells us the strength of the current trend, indicates prices where we may enter or add to a position, and once the previous peak/trough is exceeded, these retracement levels may be used for our stop placement.

Section II

Using Retracement Theory to Trade

Chapter 1

Conventional Uses of the Relative Strength Index

Before continuing, here is a brief review of the published literature regarding how to conventionally use the Relative Strength Index. This information is important because it serves to highlight the reasons why so many people fail to make money in trading. Since most of the published literature has little value, it serves us to show us what NOT to do or believe in. In this section, my comments are indented.

When Welles Wilder introduced the RSI, he recommended using a 14-period look-back when using daily data. The RSI is actually a momentum indicator that follows the price activity of an underlying security. Because of the structure of the formula, the RSI value is contained between a minimum value of 0 and a maximum value of 100. The RSI formula was developed almost 30 years ago. As a result, certain beliefs have developed over the years as to how to best use this versatile indicator. Welles Wilder described some of these beliefs in his original work and different traders through their collective experience with the indicator have developed other beliefs. There are 9 basic beliefs concerning the best way to use the RSI:

1. Indication of Tops and Bottoms
2. Divergence
3. Failure Swings
4. Support and Resistance Levels
5. RSI Chart Formations

6. Altman Modified - Smoothed RSI
7. Morris Modified RSI
8. Modification of Look Back Period
9. Modification of the Data Source Used

1. Indication of Tops and Bottoms

In many cases, the RSI value will "top out" in the range above 70 and "bottom out" in the range below 30. RSI tops and bottoms often precede price tops and bottoms. The RSI begins making tops and bottoms before they become obvious on a price chart. Many traders use the 30 level as a buy zone and the 70 level as a sell zone. Some traders have modified these values to make the buy zone 20 and the sell zone 80.

In the past few years, this concept has been expanded. This method generates a buy or sell signal <u>only</u> when the RSI <u>leaves</u> the zone. In other words, if the RSI is 73 on Monday, 71 on Tuesday, and 68 on Wednesday, Wednesday is <u>now</u> a bearish indication, telling us to go short on the open Thursday. If the RSI in the last bar is under 30, we would get an indication to buy when the current bar closes with the RSI rising above 30. This is <u>now</u> a bullish signal to get long on the open of the next bar.

The top and bottom levels recommended by Wilder are 70 and 30. However, there is published information that advises modifying these RSI levels if the price is trending higher or lower. While some traders consider an RSI value of 70 a sell signal, the number would be revised to 80 if prices were in an uptrend. If the prices are trending lower, the buy zone would be changed from an RSI value of 30 to 20.

> *JH: Basing a trading methodology on this principal will only lead to losses.*

2. Divergence

This is the most popular use of the RSI. Bearish Divergence occurs when the RSI value fails to make a new high as the price is making a new high. A Bullish Divergence occurs when a new low in price is made while the RSI value is not making a new low. The price action is diverging from the RSI action. Whenever price action is trending up and the RSI values are trending down, you are seeing a "Bearish Divergence." Whenever you see prices trending lower and the RSI values trending higher, you are seeing a "Bullish Divergence."

When a divergence is encountered on a chart, the accepted belief is that a reversal in price is imminent. Published literature also states that the most powerful divergence occurs when many time periods or bars have elapsed. The time period number for these strong divergences is anywhere from 30 to 90 bars.

> *JH: Going long when a bullish divergence makes its appearance is a certain way to make small profits and generate large losses!*

3. Failure Swings

This concept is actually a part of divergence. A failure swing occurs when there is either a bearish or bullish divergence. By looking at Chart #3, you can more easily see a failure swing. As the price makes a new low, the RSI fails to make a new low so a bullish divergence is formed. The next day prices rally causing the RSI value to also rally. When the RSI value exceeds its previous peak, it is called a "failure swing." It typically indicates that prices will continue to move higher. A failure swing with a bearish divergence is the same type formation only the RSI moves lower than the previous trough. This is a failure swing down. The failure swing is believed to "confirm" that a market reversal is valid.

> *JH: A failure swing only confirms that the divergence is real. Waiting to go long until a failure swing occurs after a divergence makes its appearance is a sure way to make small profits and generate large losses!*

CHART # 3 – FAILURE SWING

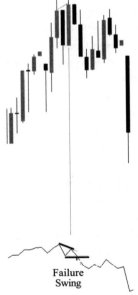

Failure
Swing

4. **Support and Resistance levels**

The RSI chart can be used to more clearly see support and resistance levels. In addition, many traders use the 50 level as support and/or resistance. When the RSI rallies from under 50 to above 50, it is considered a bullish confirmation. When the RSI crosses from above 50 to below 50, this is seen as bearish confirmation.

JH: It pays to notice when the RSI crosses 50, but this should not be our main focus while trading! We know that the RSI crosses the 50 level when the ratio of up days to down days averages reverse.

5. **RSI Chart Formations**

There are many times when RSI values make triangles, pennants, double tops and bottoms, or head and shoulders patterns that are not visible on a price chart. The RSI lends itself to the use of trendlines and horizontal support and resistance lines on the chart. The validity of these lines is the same as that on a price chart.

JH: This is absolutely true! The most common pattern is the triangle formation, which often indicates a pending explosive move. However,
→ *there is often a false breakout before the real move!*

6. **Altman Modified RSI (commonly called RMI)**

Roger Altman modified the RSI formula to reflect more of a momentum aspect. He believed that the RSI oscillated inconsistently between overbought and oversold levels. While the RSI calculates the change in gain/loss "bar to bar," Mr. Altman modified the formula to calculate the change from the "n'th" bar in the past (where n is more than 1). This modification is referred to as the RMI or Relative Momentum Index. Some traders like it because it smoothes the zigzag appearance of the RSI. This defeats the purpose of using the RSI to obtain an early indication of important price behaviors as it introduces time lag into the calculation. When I want to smooth the RSI, I like to use a smoothing constant of 3 with a look back period of 14. The literature recommends using 7, 9, 14, or 25 as a smoothing constant.

JH: We will not use this method in creating trading rules. There is a lot that can be done with this concept and it might be a good idea to explore some variations once you understand the concepts in this book. By using a smoothing constant, we are introducing time lag into our analysis, which we do not want for the purposes of this book. However, once we learn about Momentum Discrepancy Reversal Points, RMI can be used as a filter. By applying a smoothing constant of 3, many of the more "fine" distinctions such as a 2-period Bear divergence would be eliminated. The appearance of either a Momentum Discrepancy Reversal Point or divergence will have added significance and validity with the RMI. Once you have mastered the RSI, come back to the RMI and compare its performance in real time versus the RSI. I suspect that you may like what you find.

CHART # 4 – COMPARISON OF RSI (BOTTOM) VS. RMI
(TOP - WITH A SMOOTHING CONSTANT OF 3)

7. **Morris Modified RSI**

This derivative of the Wilder RSI was introduced in the 1998 Bonus issue of *Stocks & Commodities Magazine*. The Wilder formula uses an exponential moving average on the second bar after the look back period. The Morris RSI continues to calculate the average gain and average loss on the last "n" bars but it calculates the indicator with a simple moving average. Changing the calculation in this way increases the volatility and generates more buy and sell signals because it crosses the 70 and 30 levels more frequently.

JH: For the purposes of this book, we will not use this modified RSI. Perhaps the best use for this modified formula is in detecting hidden signals. As the smoothing component of the RSI has been eliminated, the signal line will be much more "jagged" generating more hidden divergence signals and Momentum Discrepancy Reversal Points and simple bullish and bearish divergence.

CHART # 5 – COMPARISON OF MORRIS MODIFIED RSI (MIDDLE PANEL) VERSUS RSI (BOTTOM PANEL)

8. **Modification of the Look-Back Period**

By modifying the look-back period used in the RSI calculation, it is possible to make the RSI <u>more</u> or <u>less</u> volatile. Decreasing the look-back period increases the RSI volatility while increasing the look-back period reduces the volatility. As the volatility changes, the RSI "the range" of top and bottom value also changes. Some traders change the look-back period causing the RSI to oscillate within a certain band. Should the trader want the RSI value to be very sensitive to price change, then they want to use a shorter look-back period. Many traders use a 9 and 25-bar look-back period plus a 14 period look-back.

> *JH: The common reason to do this is to gain a perspective of a different timeframe. This is better accomplished by using a 14 period look-back RSI on charts that use different units of time.*

CHART # 6 – COMPARISON OF **RSI** (3 BAR LOOK-BACK) AND **RSI** (14 BAR LOOK-BACK)

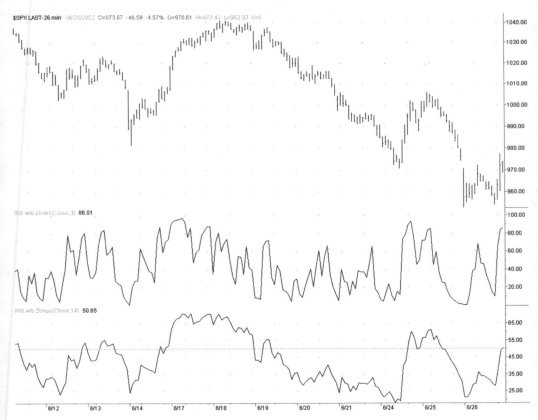

Chart 6 Comments:
This chart illustrates how much easier the RSI 3 bar look back (middle panel) can be driven to overbought or oversold levels.

9.   Modification of the Data Source
Traders have also used the RSI formula by using the change in the open, high or low price rather than the closing price in the calculation. An alternative to using the closing price is to apply a formula that manipulates the price in a certain way and applying the RSI formula to this synthetic number. Some of the price modifications are to determine the average of the High/Low, Open/Close, Open Yesterday/Close Today or any other variation of range.

One of the more novel approaches is to determine the standard deviation of the close over the previous 10 days and base the RSI upon how the standard deviation changes each day. This variation is an alternative way to measure market strength.

> *JH: I like this concept. It is an alternative and very effective way to measure market strength. However because the purpose of this book is to gain a thorough understanding of the RSI, it will not be discussed further. Once you understand the concepts included in this book, take some time to play with this idea. As you will see in Chart #7 below, whenever the RSI modified value exceeds 70, the internal strength of the market is overextended. To use this indicator, it is easiest to think that when the value is over 70, the "Duracell Bunny" has no energy left to push prices higher or lower. For the "Duracell Bunny" to push prices, he must retreat to under 40 to recharge his batteries!*

CHART # 7 – RSI 14 PERIOD (MIDDLE PANEL) VERSUS RSI STANDARD DEVIATION (BOTTOM PANEL)

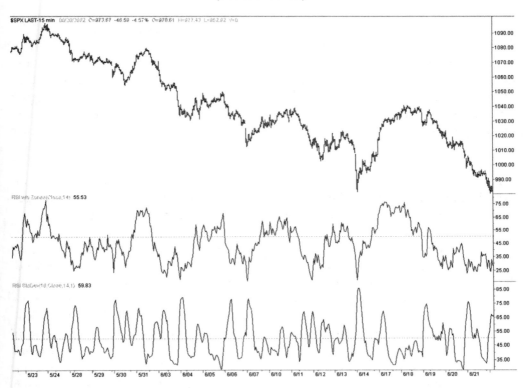

Summary of Published Literature

Unfortunately, if a trader relied on these commonly accepted methodologies to trade with the Relative Strength Index, he or she would probably lose all of their money! The most powerful ways to use the RSI are not even described in the published literature!

CHAPTER 2

PROFESSIONAL RSI USE

As discussed in the previous section, these are the nine widely known methods to use the RSI:

1. Indication of Tops and Bottoms
2. Divergence
3. Failure Swings
4. Support and Resistance Levels
5. RSI Chart Formations
6. Altman Modified - Smoothed RSI
7. Morris Modified RSI
8. Modification of Look Back Period
9. Modification of the Data Source

In the beginning of this book, I mentioned that we would use the RSI to identify:

1. The current trend – if any.
2. Best prices to enter or exit a trade.
3. Price levels for probable retracement.
4. The dominant timeframe.
5. When a longer timeframe is negating or overpowering the present timeframe.
6. Price objectives that have a high probability of success.

I understand that many traders who are reading this book are probably confused, especially if they have studied the "conventional" uses of the RSI. The confusion comes because I am telling you that using the RSI as an indicator of tops and bottoms "as described" is wrong. I have said that using the RSI for divergence recognition and

55

order entry will generate losses and that using the RSI to indicate a bullish or bearish bias when the RSI is above or below the 50 level will generate further loses. These statements go against the "conventional" trading ideas that are associated with the interpretation of the RSI.

In order to use any indicator correctly, a trader must thoroughly understand it. Once the indicator is understood, it must be accepted as it is. "It is what it is." For example, it doesn't matter that "everyone" is saying that tops occur at 70 and bottoms occur at 30, if this rarely happens. Many traders when using an indicator get caught in a trap of thinking "could've, should've, would've." Traders who use conventional RSI knowledge are often frustrated because they believe that the market "should've" done this because the RSI is doing "that."

The 10 RSI Lies that Traders Believe:

1. A bearish divergence is an indication that an uptrend is about to end
2. A bullish divergence is an indication that a downtrend is about to end
3. The RSI will generally "top out" somewhere around the 70 level. At this point, we want to start thinking of getting short or at the very least exiting long trades.
4. That the RSI will generally "bottom out" somewhere around the 30 level. At this point, we want to start thinking of getting long or at the very least exiting short trades.
5. Whenever the RSI is above 50, it is a bullish indication. If not long, find an excuse to get long.
6. Whenever the RSI is below 50, it's a bearish indication. If not short, find a reason to get short.
7. A failure swing is a significant event.
8. The RSI is unable to indicate trend direction, because it's only a momentum indicator.
9. The RSI is unable to indicate trend reversals, because it's only a momentum indicator.
10. It is not possible to use the RSI to set price objectives.

In this section, we are going to use everything covered in Section I to begin using the RSI to consistently generate profits. The amount of profit and the consistency of the profits are dependent upon the quality of your analysis and your psychological resources. If you are interested, I have written a book devoted to the best ways to increase your psychological resources. It is entitled *The 21 Irrefutable Truths of Trading*. By the end of this book, the quality of your analysis will have improved significantly and you will be able to determine the following <u>without looking at the bars on a price chart</u>:

1. The current trend.
2. When the current trend will probably retrace.
3. When the current retracement is no longer a retracement but a trend reversal.
4. The best time and price to enter or exit a trade.
5. Support and resistance numbers for accurate stop placement.
6. High probability price objectives helping to establish risk/reward parameters.
7. When a longer timeframe or traders with more capitalization have entered the marketplace.

CHAPTER 3

TREND DETERMINATION UING RSI

The traders' eternal question of "What is the trend?" is easily answered when a trader knows how to interpret the RSI. A trend is supposed to be easy to describe, but for many traders it is very difficult to identify in real time. Up trends are defined as prices making higher highs, and retracement lows or troughs are higher as well. A downtrend is the inverse.

Just as an uptrend, downtrend or sideways price action is visible on a price chart, the same behavior can be seen on the RSI chart. You can see chart examples of the RSI making a higher top, retracing to make a low that does not exceed the previous low, followed by a rally to a new high establishing the pattern of an uptrend.

There are many times that the RSI will show an uptrend or downtrend that is not obvious on the price chart. The chart below on the left will illustrate this concept. It is a slice from a 15-minute chart of the E-Mini S&P on May 13, 2002. We can see that the RSI is making higher highs and higher lows. Looking at the price bars, it is easy to see that prices are rising. However, it isn't so easy to see the market retracements. Clearly, the market is trending higher.

CHART # 8 – 15 MINUTE CHART & CHART # 9 – 1 MINUTE CHART E-MINI S&P

Using this concept will identify the trend *using the RSI in a timeframe that is shorter than the one you are studying.* In the 15-minute chart to the left, the price is trending up, but placing a trade based on this 15-minute chart using the RSI would be difficult because there is no clear place to buy unless you are using a breakout strategy. One of the problems with breakout strategies is that they often experience considerable price slippage. Our goal is to enter our trades on limit orders when the market retraces some of the previous move. In this example, if we were 1-minute timeframe traders using the 15-minute chart for confirmation, we would be able to find multiple entry points on the 1-minute chart on the right. The 15-minute chart on the left serves as a trend confirmation tool.

There is a better way to use the RSI. In the mathematical chapter of Section 1, we discussed how the ratio between the up average and the down average affects the RSI value. The RSI behaves like a logarithmic function. This causes the largest changes in the RSI value to occur when the up/down average stays in the range of ratios between 1:2 to 2:1. This range of ratios corresponds to RSI values from 33.33 to 66.67. Do you recognize the Fibonacci number? It is in this band of values that we see the largest movement of the RSI value versus change in price. This is why the conventional knowledge states that tops typically occur around an RSI value of 70 and bottoms will occur around 30.

Looking at any chart with the RSI, we can see multiple times when tops were around 70 and bottoms were around 30. Within that overall chart picture, the price behavior may have been trending up, down, sideways or some combination. A very well established fact is that markets can become very emotional causing prices to exceed a "fair" level before retracing. The RSI will also push too high or too low before retracing.

Chart # 10 demonstrates an up trending market that is being dominated by 5-minute traders. The price and RSI are moving steadily higher. The retracements are clearly visible in both the RSI and price. The RSI value is easily exceeding the 70 level and is staying well above the 30 level. Closer examination reveals that the RSI is staying above 40 once the trend begins.

Chart # 10 – 5 minute S&P E-Mini 5/13/02—Uptrend

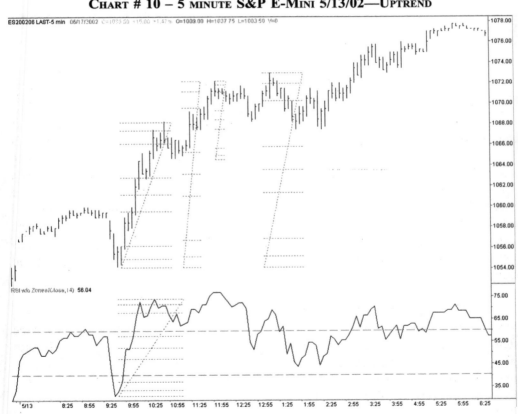

Chart # 11 shows a market that has started to trend lower being dominated by 5-minute traders. The chart shows the RSI often falling below the RSI value of 30 and that it is not exceeding the 70 level on rallies. Closer examination of the chart reveals that the RSI is not getting over the 60 level and at times is having a hard time moving above 40. This is a great indication that the market is going much lower.

CHART # 11 – 5 MINUTE S&P E-MINI 6/25/02—DOWNTREND

This chart reveals an interesting observation. In an uptrending market (Chart 10), the RSI value does not go under the 33.33 level and <u>often</u> stays above the 40 level while routinely exceeding the 70 level. In downtrends (Chart 11), the RSI doesn't go above the 66.67 level and often stays <u>under</u> 60 while routinely going under the 33.33 level. At this point, we can make a general observation that in an uptrend 33.33 is support and 66.66 is resistance in a downtrend.

Referring back to the ratio Table # 3 on page 10, once the up/down ratio climbs to 4:1 or 1:4, the incremental increase or decrease of the RSI value has rapidly decreased. We can observe that the <u>majority</u> of the RSI movement will fall within these boundaries. Significant mathematical resistance is encountered at an RSI value of 80 and significant support is encountered at a value of 20. This is not exactly what everyone else says!

As we can see in an uptrend, support is 33.33 - not 20. In a downtrend, resistance is 66.67 - not 80. By combining everything and knowing that prices and the RSI can become "hysterical," we can come up with the following rules:

<u>Rule #1</u>
1. In uptrends, the RSI will find support at 33.33 and resistance at 80.
2. In downtrends, the RSI will find resistance at 66.67, and support at 20.

Rule # 1 is illustrated in Charts # 10 and 11.

Careful examination of thousands of charts reveals that support in an uptrending market is closer to 40 than to 33 and resistance in a down trending market is closer to 60 than 67. However, these levels are only valid when the <u>majority of traders</u> in the marketplace all are focusing on the same timeframe. If there are traders focused on a different timeframe, they may cause these significant levels to be momentarily negated without destroying the trend.

Using the 80/40 and 60/20 range rules, we can instantly identify the trend the majority of the time. If the RSI is staying within the 80/40 ranges, we know that the trend is up, and the majority of the "other" traders are also looking at this same time frame. If the RSI is staying within the 60/20 ranges, we know that the Bears are in control and the trend is down. Just understanding this one rule allows us to quickly determine the trend without looking at a price chart! Then, by adding our knowledge of basic retracement theory, we can confirm the RSI behavior by observing the depth of the retracements on the price bars. Should traders in a longer timeframe take interest in our timeframe, then the RSI levels will not be respected and we can expect to see deep retracements. RSI and price "behavior" will tell us if the preceding trend is still in effect or if the trend has in all probability changed. Before we can discuss this price behavior, we must first understand some more RSI concepts. In Chart #4, the 40 level did not prove to be support as it was negated by a longer timeframe, but the bull market was still intact.

<u>Rule #1 – Modified</u>
1. In an uptrend, the RSI finds resistance at 80 and support at 40.
2. In a downtrend, the RSI finds resistance at 60 and support at 20.

CHART # 12 – BULL MARKET WHERE 40 WAS NEGATED AND BULL TREND REMAINED INTACT.

CHAPTER 4

THE TRUTH ABOUT DIVERGENCE

One of the first things that every trader learns early in his or her career is the concept of divergence. Whenever divergence is discussed, it seems that the majority of examples used to illustrate the concept use the Relative Strength Index. Divergence occurs in any momentum-based indicator and occurs when price and an indicator are doing different things, i.e., price is moving higher and the indicator is moving lower or vice versa. These types of divergence are classified as <u>simple divergence</u>. There are also examples of multiple long-term divergence and hidden divergence.

CHART # 13 – THE RISE OF INTEL – WHERE IS THE BULLISH DIVERGENCE?

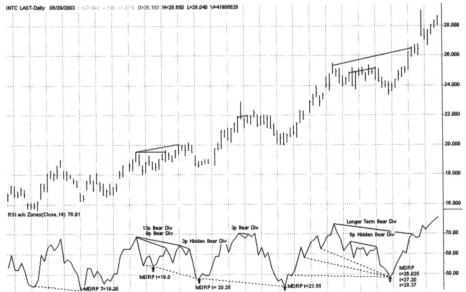

Chart # 13 Note:
Don't worry about what a MDRP is for now. Focus on finding the Bullish Divergence in this bullish chart. There are none! We shall see that they only occur in bear markets, not bull markets!

Let's examine the concept behind a bullish divergence.

First. What is the price behavior doing just before a <u>bullish divergence</u> occurs on a chart? Price is declining. As more traders realize that the price is heading lower, they are attempting to get short or exit their longs by selling. The majority of these orders are "at the market," and the floor brokers and traders continue to lower their offers to buy since the majority of the order flow is "at the market." In other words, the sellers are hitting the buyers offer price causing the floor traders who are buying to continually lower their bid. Each time a new trade is executed the bid price drops.

Second. The RSI very accurately reflects the change in the average gain or loss for a time period. As prices continue to fall, they very often begin to accelerate lower. This acceleration is reflected in the RSI. The RSI value falls below 40, below 33.33, then below 30. At this point from our previous study of the ratios, we know that the ratio of average loss to average gain is badly extended. As the RSI moves lower, it is encountering increasing mathematical resistance. Remember that the RSI is a logarithmic line and for it to move lower when it is below the 30 level is much more difficult than when it was at 50.

Third. As prices continue to fall, one or two things will happen. The more perceptive traders in the existing timeframe realize that prices are becoming overextended. These are the traders who got short early in the decline. They begin buying to exit their positions and help to slow the plunge. As the plunge slows, the somewhat less perceptive traders also realize that prices are overextended and they also begin to exit, which typically stops the decline. Concurrently, traders in a longer timeframe may have realized that prices are too low and step in with their buy orders. As soon as the plunge stops and prices begin to rally, even the dumb (but not proud) traders realize that the plunge is over and begin buying propelling prices higher.

What was the cause for prices to accelerate downward in the first place? The answer to this question is simple; there were no buyers in the market. In order for the sell "at market" orders to be filled, someone had to be willing to buy. If there are many sell orders and no buyers, then prices can only go down. If there are no sell or buy orders entering the pit, prices will stagnate.

In any case, prices stop declining and begin to rally at some point. Just as an air bubble expands in size as it ascends in liquid, the RSI expands upward as it moves up from its extremely compressed state at the 30 or lower level. This is ordained because of its mathematical formula. As prices rally, there will be traders who begin to think that prices are "too" high and begin to sell; pushing prices lower thereby making new lows.

Because the RSI uses a ratio of average gain to average loss over "N" periods of time, it will be forced lower, *but at a lesser rate than its previous rate of increase.* Consequently, we will see a new low price, but the RSI value will not see a lower value than its previous low. This is a divergence between price and the RSI. At some point, the Bulls will overpower the Bears and the market will see another rally. Because the RSI value is so compressed, it will begin to increase its acceleration higher. As the RSI rises from levels below 30 towards 40, it begins to incrementally increase more than the price increases, giving the <u>illusion</u> of a new low.

The important question is, "Did the RSI rally above the 66.7 level or more generally the 60 level?" If not – the trend is still down. Let me ask you, "When does a bullish divergence make its appearance on the RSI chart?" The answer is only when prices have been declining. If divergence is considered within the context of trend, what is the existing trend when we see a bullish divergence? A downtrend! What can we use as an indication that the trend is down? We know we are in a downtrend when we see a bullish divergence. This is why in the above Intel chart there are no Bullish Divergences – the market is trending higher, NOT lower!

I realize that the published trading literature states that a bullish divergence is an indication that prices are about to rally. The "implication" is that a bullish divergence is an indication that an <u>uptrend</u> is about to commence. As you are now realizing, a bullish divergence only appears when the <u>existing trend is down</u>. If the trend is clearly down, why are we even thinking of buying? Wouldn't it be more prudent to be looking for a place to get short?

A bullish divergence signifies that the existing trend is down and the Bears are exhausted. We should be expecting a rally to sell into. If we have short positions, then we should exit some or all of the shorts, <u>but not reverse to become long!</u> Prices should rally or reverse to some degree before falling to new lows.

Inversely, when we see a bearish divergence, the trend is up and we should probably expect a retracement to lower prices because the Bulls are exhausted. It is time that we should begin looking for a reason to buy.

<u>A simple divergence means that prices have encountered enough resistance that they need time to consolidate their previous move. Once this has occurred, prices will resume their downward or upward march.</u>

The price that generated the divergence often becomes a key number used to identify temporary support or resistance. Once this price is negated, it becomes a resistance or support point and can be used for a stop price.

CHART 14—DIVERGENCE PRICE BECOMING FUTURE RESISTANCE OR SUPPORT

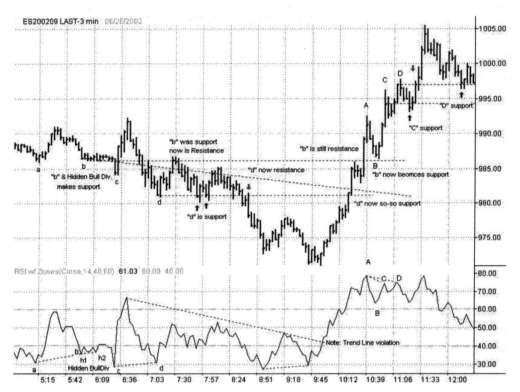

Chart 14 Notes:

This chart contains 2 bullish divergence and one bearish divergence. The price where the divergence was made became future support/resistance. Remember that support once negated often becomes resistance and vice versa.

The strength of a divergence formation can be determined by observing the number of time bars that have elapsed between the RSI peaks and troughs that are creating the divergence. This is called Divergence Strength and is a method that is used to rank divergence as strong or weak. Generally, if the number of time intervals is less than 4, then there is strength in the divergence and an immediate retracement should occur. As the number of time intervals increases, the likelihood of a retracement decreases. In Chart #14, from point C to point A there are 6 bars. This is called a 6 period

Bearish Divergence and is not very potent. In the Intel Chart #13 the interval is indicated by 'N'p.

As the time interval between the RSI peaks and troughs increases, the likelihood of seeing <u>multiple divergences</u> also increases. Multiple bearish divergences occur when there are successively higher price rallies while the RSI has successive lower rally highs. Here is <u>the paradox of divergences; simple divergence provides a strong indication that the preceding trend will resume as soon as the retracement is completed.</u> But, multiple long-term divergences increase the likelihood that the preceding trend has ended. This concept is illustrated below in Chart #15.

CHART # 15 – LONG-TERM MULTIPLE BULLISH DIVERGENCE

In Chart #15, there are three bullish divergences where the price has made three consecutive lower lows while the RSI made three consecutive higher lows. These higher bullish divergences would be classified as multiple long-term bullish divergences. They are indicating that there is an increasing probability of a trend reversal occurring.

The most powerful divergence signals are called <u>hidden divergences</u>. They are called hidden divergences because they are not obvious to the untrained trader. These divergences do not occur at the bottom or top of the RSI chart like their more common cousins. They appear after the RSI has either rallied (bullish hidden divergence) or after the RSI has dropped from its high (bearish hidden divergence). Hidden divergence typically occurs in the 40 to 60 ranges. When hidden divergence occurs, it is classified as the strongest divergence possible. The market will do <u>exactly</u> as the name indicates. A hidden bullish divergence is a very strong indication that prices are about to strongly rally. Put another way, a hidden bullish divergence that appears in a bear market is a strong indication that the trend is about to reverse. Chart #16 shows hidden bullish divergence. You can also see a 3p Hidden Bear Divergence in Chart #13 of Intel.

CHART # 16 — HIDDEN BULLISH DIVERGENCE

In Chart #16 Note a hidden bullish divergence showed up beneath the 30 level after a 9 period simple bullish divergence. Immediately after forming the pattern, prices had a significant bear rally. Notice that the Bears stopped the advance when the RSI value approached 60.

Building a chart that combines a 9 period RSI and a 9 period Stochastic Indicator (slow) is a method that can be used to identify strong multiple divergences indicating strong contra-trend retracements or possible trend reversals. The exact pattern that we are looking for is three or more simultaneous long-term divergences in the RSI and Stochastic charts. When this occurs, you not only exit your position but reverse positions by taking a smaller than normal position 1 or 2 ticks above the high or low of the second peak or trough.

CHART # 17 – RSI & STOCHASTIC WITH 3 SIMULTANEOUS BULL DIVERGENCES

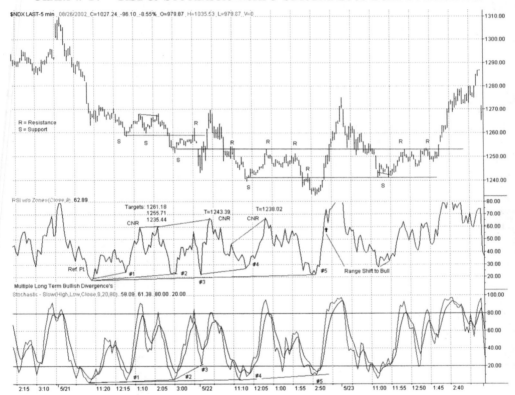

Chart #17 Notes:

In the RSI, we have multiple medium term bullish divergences at: 1 (against the reference point) and 3 (using 4 as a reference point). We have long-term multiple divergences at: 2, 3, and 5 all against the reference point. Point # 4 is not a long-term multiple divergence as it is not under #3 and above the reference point. In the Slow Stochastic, we have medium term bullish divergences at 1 (against the reference point), 2 (using 1 as a reference point) and 3 (using 2 as a reference point). We have multiple long-term divergences at 2, 4, and 5 (all against the reference point). Point #3 is not a long-term bullish divergence for the same reason #4 in the RSI was not.

71

I added some information to this chart regarding MDRP DOWN signals. We will discuss these signals in the next section. What is noteworthy is that we were able to project downside targets that were eventually hit. This entire time, we did not see any bearish divergences and the RSI stayed under 60. I marked the chart showing when the Bulls were able to gain control when they were able to push the RSI above 60. Also, take note of the semi-hidden bullish signal on May 23, 2002 around 11:30. We can see how the price that coincides with the divergence point often becomes future support or resistance, which will be useful with our stop placement.

End of Chart # 17 Notes.

As in life, there are exceptions to every rule. With the exception of three or more long-term bearish/bullish divergences and hidden divergences, the appearance of a simple divergence is a very strong indication that the trend is <u>opposite</u> of what the name implies. When a simple divergence is encountered, the only trade strategy that can be employed is to exit some (or all) of the trade position. Once prices begin to retrace the preceding trend and a contra-trend move or retracement is seen, the price that coincides with the RSI peak or trough becomes a key price. This price will often prove to be temporary support/resistance once the preceding trend re-asserts itself. Once the price has negated this temporary support, this price area may be used as a stop.

<u>Rule # 3:</u>
An Uptrend is indicated when:
1. RSI values remain in an 80/40 range
2. The chart exhibits simple bearish divergence
3. Hidden bullish divergence are seen

A Downtrend is indicated when:
1. RSI values remain in a 60/20 range
2. The chart exhibits simple bullish divergence
3. Hidden bearish divergence is seen

Chapter 5

Momentum Discrepancy Reversal Points

The RSI behaves at times in a manner that indicates prices have retraced part of their preceding move too quickly. When this occurs, the shorter timeframe traders have overextended themselves in the retracement. If prices on a 5-minute chart were rallying in a strong uptrend and the 5-minute traders became overextended, prices would begin retracing some of the prior move in a contra-trend retracement to the down side. However, as prices headed lower, they would become overextended because of the 1-minute timeframe traders. Since the RSI is a very sensitive momentum based indicator, it has the ability to detect these hysterical overextended retracements.

When the RSI retracement exceeds the previous peak or trough and price has not exceeded its previous peak or trough, this is called a Momentum Discrepancy Reversal Point. Andrew Cardwell discovered this pattern and has taught many traders how to recognize and implement this pattern into their overall trading strategy.

Momentum Discrepancy Reversal Up – MDRP UP for the Bulls!

This pattern only occurs when the Bulls are pushing prices higher in a bullish trend. Occasionally, prices will retrace some of the previous rally, while staying above a prior price trough. The RSI simultaneously retraces <u>beyond</u> a previous RSI trough where the price that coincides with this RSI trough is lower than the current price. This is a Momentum Discrepancy Reversal Up (MDRP UP). Described another way, a Momentum Discrepancy Reversal Up (MDRP UP) occurs when the RSI value is lower than a prior RSI trough, and the price is higher. Until the RSI "hooks up," the formation is a "tentative" MDRP UP. Once the RSI has hooked to the upside, the formation is a "locked in" MDRP UP. The price that coincides with this trough is a <u>significant price</u>. Chart #18 illustrates this concept:

CHART # 18 – MOMENTUM DISCREPANCY REVERSAL POINT UP

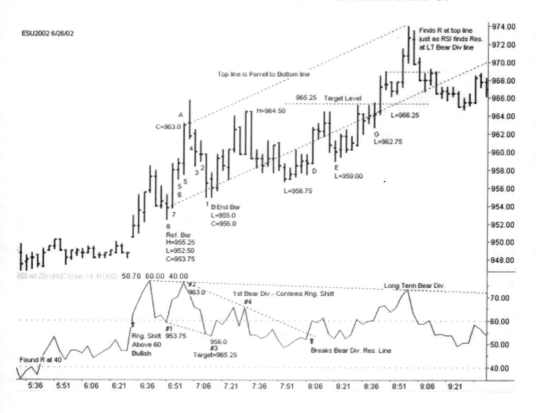

Chart # 18 Notes:

This is a 3-minute chart of the E-Mini S&P 500 from June 26, 2002. Early in the trading day, the market was bearish because the RSI value was under 40. There was a small rally and resistance was encountered at RSI 40 value. Normally, this is a good indication that the market is about to get hammered. In this case, the market made a 3 period bullish divergence at 8:39. When the cash market opened at 9:30, the Bulls made a small opening gap pushing prices higher, negating the RSI 60 level. At this point, we know that the trend has probably changed to UP. We receive confirmation of this when the RSI retraces lower and finds support at 60 (#1 on the RSI chart and the "Ref" bar on the price chart). The ensuing rally found prices at point "A" before retracing lower to point "B" on the price chart. At this point, we see that the RSI value is lower at point "B" than at point "A," but the price is higher. This formation is a Momentum Discrepancy Reversal Up (MDRP UP).

74

We can calculate the strength by determining the number of bars preceding point "B." In this case, it is an 8 period MDRP UP, which is a medium strong signal. Like the strength indication of a divergence signal, the strongest Momentum Discrepancy Reversal Point signals are 2 to 4 periods in length. A medium strength signal is 5 to 15 time periods and a weak signal is anything over 16 time periods. We can also calculate the upside target by obtaining the difference between points "B" and "Ref" and adding the difference to point "A."

$$(956.00 - 953.75) + 963.0 = 965.25$$

The next question that arises is where do we get long? We must consider our risk to reward ratio that we ideally want to be a minimum of 1:3. Since the close of bar "B" was 956.0 and our upside target is 965.25, our potential profit is 9.25 points. To maintain our risk to reward ratio, we must risk no more than 3.0 points. My preference is to not risk more than one point on a 3 minute S&P trade. We need to find a point to exit the trade in the event the Momentum Discrepancy Reversal Up fails. Careful examination of the chart shows that the high for the "Ref" bar was 955.25 and the low of bars "1" and "B" were both 955.00. This would be a double bottom in a timeframe that is smaller than 3 minutes. We can surmise that the Bulls will probably protect 955.00, so our stop can be placed at 954.75. Since we are trading in a 3-minute time window, the odds of using a limit order, which is the preferred method, to enter the trade are not very good because of the double bottom. Because of this, we should enter a "buy at market" order, which will get us long at approximately 956.00 with a stop placed at 954.75.

We could have entered one bar earlier at bar "1" because with the close of bar "1," we had a MDRP UP which can be seen by carefully looking at the RSI chart. See how the downward slant changes just before the ultimate low? If we had observed this, we could have entered a buy limit order at 955.25 with a stop placed at 954.75. The reason that the low was made in bar "1" was because the traders in a smaller timeframe saw the high at 955.25, which was resistance at that time. When that point was negated, it should become support. The traders in the smaller timeframe entered their buy orders at 955.25. With the close above the previous close in bar "C," the formation is a "locked in" MDRP UP. We can move our stop to 955.75, which is a tick below the close of 956.00.

At this point, we are long and want to maximize our profits on this trade. The upside target for this trade is 965.25. Prices rally to a high of 964.5 closing on the high of the bar, which is a bullish sign. In the next bar, prices collapse and the high is the same as the open, which is a very bearish sign. Prices were within 0.75 points of our target. With the collapse in prices, we have a bear divergence, making two medium term divergences. We do not have a long-term bearish divergence as the RSI at (#4) is not above (#2) and below the RSI peak.

Since prices must close at or above the target to confirm the bull market, we should be somewhat nervous about ever seeing a profit. The Bears push prices down to a low of 956.75 before the Bulls begin to buy again. Our stop is still at 955.75 and we are still long the market. As the Bulls begin to push prices higher, we begin trailing our stop higher. Why didn't we trail our stop earlier? When we entered the trade, all indications were that prices were headed higher. Once we begin trailing our protective stop, the probability of being stopped out in a minor retracement increases. So we wait for the first minor retracement before moving our initial stop.

The reason that we began using a trailing stop is because prices should have reached our target and didn't! With the close on bar "D," we have confirmation that the Bulls are going to push prices higher. How do we know this? "D" is the first bar since the low of 956.75 where the Bulls managed to close a 3-minute bar above the high of *the preceding bar*. After the close of "D," we can move our stop from 955.75 to 956.50, which is one tick below the low. This is not much, but every little bit helps. The Bulls once again rally prices before faltering and retracing to "E". The next bar after "E" sees the Bulls closing the bar above the high of bar "E" confirming the validity of the Bulls intentions and the swing point low of "E." We can move our stop from 956.50 to 958.75.

The Bulls rally prices to our target price of 965.25. The price just touches it before closing under it at bar "F." In all probability, our sell limit order of 956.25 would not have been filled. However, three bars later at bar "G," the Bulls extend prices to just above 965.25 before closing the bar out under it. With bar "H," we finally achieved our upside target of 965.25! With bar "G" pushing prices just above 965.25, we could have exited our trade with a "sell 965.25 or better" order. If our position had only one lot, that is what we should have done. If our position had multiple contracts, we should have exited 50% of our trades and kept the rest of the position in case the trade turned into a big winner.

Assuming that we had multiple positions, we would be long with the close of bar "H." We need to move our trailing stop to just under the latest swing low at bar "G." The price level for the stop is 962.75. Naturally, the Bulls encounter resistance after the next bar after "H." We had an idea that there would be resistance at this level because there was a fairly large upper shadow in "H." Prices retrace lower in the next two bars making a low at "I" before rallying again. With the second bar after "I," we can move our stop from 962.75 to 966.00.

The question that naturally arises is "Where do we exit our remaining position?" Previously, we discussed that trendlines on the RSI chart are as strong as trendlines on the price chart. The problem with drawing trendlines on price charts is that their placement is largely subjective. Ask 100 technical analysts to draw trendlines on the same chart and you will get 100 different trendlines! By using the RSI, very accurate trendlines can be drawn. We can draw a valid trendline whenever we can identify a Momentum Discrepancy Reversal Point. In Chart #18, we have the bottom trendline, which is based on the Close of the "Ref" bar and the Close of bar "B." After drawing this trendline, we can draw a parallel trendline and place it on the highest Close between the reference and end bar of the Momentum Discrepancy Reversal Point pattern. You can see this bar in Chart #18. We will discuss RSI and MRDP point based trendlines on page 80.

When prices rallied to the upper trendline at bar "K," we should have exited our remaining position. Should you have kept one contract "just in case" prices continued on their rocket trajectory, you should have exited the last contract when the swing low point "I" was negated 2 bars after "I." Additional emphasis should have been placed on exiting the remainder of the position when the upper trendline was negated because we were also seeing a very bearish long-term divergence in the RSI and multiple long-term bear divergences in the Stochastic indicator that is not shown.

End of Chart #18 comments.

MOMENTUM DISCREPANCY REVERSAL DOWN — MDRP DOWN FOR THE BEARS!

A Momentum Discrepancy Reversal Down (MDRP DOWN) is the exact inverse of an MDRP UP. However, I will describe it in a slightly different way to aid in clarity. As prices fall, there will be the occasional bar(s) that closes higher than the previous bar causing the RSI to generate various lower peaks. As more traders become convinced that prices will continue to fall, the plunging prices slow before reversing higher in a contra-trend rally. After all, if everybody has sold, who will continue to hit the buyers lower bids? If the bids are not being hit, then prices are unable to fall. In any case, as prices begin to rally so does the RSI. For every instance, where there was a close higher than the previous bar in the preceding downward plunge, the RSI also rallied. This gives the RSI the appearance of a jagged downward sloping line. If you remember, successive lower peaks and troughs indicate a bear market.

The RSI rallies as prices begin their contra-trend retracement higher. As the RSI rallies, the RSI value exceeds one of these previous RSI peaks and should the price that created the previous RSI peak be lower than the current price, we are seeing a "tentative" MDRP DOWN. Once the price drops and hooks the RSI down forming a peak in the RSI indicator, we have a "locked in" MDRP DOWN. This locked in MDRP DOWN gives us a <u>significant price</u> that coincides with the peak. Chart #19 illustrates this principle.

CHART #19 – MOMENTUM DISCREPANCY REVERSAL DOWN

Chart # 19 Notes:

This chart is the September 2002 30-year T-Bond futures contract. The T-Bonds rallied to make a high close of 101^27, shortly before 10:50. As it was making a high close, the RSI was generating multiple short-term bearish divergences and one long-term bearish divergence. A bearish divergence indicated that the trend was up, but the multiple bearish divergences told us that the trend was in danger of failing. With the close of 101^17 at Noon, the RSI negated the support level at 40 indicating that the uptrend was "probably over." The following rally to a close of 101^24 while the RSI stayed below 60 generated a Momentum Discrepancy Reversal Down with a downside target of 101^16. The math for this calculation is:

$$101^{17} - (101^{25} - 101^{24}) = 101^{16}$$

Since an MDRP DOWN only occurs in a bear market, we already know that the trend is down. The MDRP DOWN has a period of 19, which makes it is a weak signal. Attempting to enter the market on a limit order would not have worked

78

because after closing on the high, prices gapped lower opening the next bar at the low of the previous bar. For this reason, a market order was required. For the shorter intra-day timeframe, market orders must be used when trading with Momentum Discrepancy Reversal Points. As the timeframe expands to 30 minutes and daily bars, limit orders should be used for market entry.

Prices fell for the next two bars to Bar "C." The close at C was 101^15, which was under our downside target allowing us to exit our trade and confirming the downtrend. The next bar closed up at 101^18 and then the market fell for 2 bars, closed unchanged the next bar and rallied to make a hidden bull divergence. This formation should have been a very bullish indication, but the next bar closed below the divergence price giving us a valuable clue as to how serious the Bears were about taking prices lower. It is important to remember that when a "probable" price behavior is immediately negated, the market has just provided a very valuable piece of information.

This failure of a hidden bullish divergence raises an interesting point. When a strong indication that something is supposed to occur (in this case, prices were to "rally") and the market does the opposite of what it "should," a longer timeframe has entered the game. In effect, you are seeing and feeling the force of a longer timeframe.

The Bears pushed prices lower to 101^08 before allowing the prices to rally for two bars before pushing prices to a new low close at 101^07 making a 4 period bullish divergence. Going into the close of the trading day, the Bulls managed to rally prices to a close of 101^12. A trader who held overnight positions could have gone short on the close as prices made a MDRP DOWN with a downside target of 101^02.

When the market opened the next morning, it gapped lower. The Bulls ran prices up to close the gap and almost generated another MDRP DOWN (it would have been a MDRP DOWN if the look-back period was 9 instead of 14) before selling the market to push prices lower to a low close of 100^24. The downside target from the second MDRP DOWN had been met. Prices rallied until the RSI ran into resistance at 60 with a close of 101^04.

At this time, we had a long- term MDRP DOWN giving us a downside target of 100^20. Entering a limit order for 101^04 would have gotten us short and our stop would have been a tick above the high at 101^07. Price action proceeded to make a hidden bearish divergence, followed immediately by a hidden bullish divergence, and another hidden bearish divergence. This is highly unusual – it is a witness to the struggle be-tween the Bulls and the Bears, which the Bears won as they were the last ones to make a meaningful pattern. Prices collapsed to 100^15. The RSI made a low of 22.94 before making a bullish divergence with the close of 100^15.

End of chart # 19 notes.

DRAWING TRENDLINES BASED ON MOMENTUM DISCREPANCY REVERSAL POINTS

Looking at Charts #18 and #19, you can see that trendlines can be drawn based on the RSI and Momentum Discrepancy Reversal Points. In Chart #18, we used the upper parallel trendline as our exit point. As mentioned before, there are many methodologies used to draw trendlines. By taking our knowledge of Momentum Discrepancy Reversal Points, we can then draw very accurate and significant trendlines.

In an ideal world, a trendline represents either a floor (support) or a ceiling (resistance) that prices will only negate when the trend has actually changed. The reason that many traders are leery of entering a trade based on a trendline is because they do not know how to draw statistically significant trendlines. When a trendline is drawn using the RSI in junction with a Momentum Discrepancy Reversal Point, the "reliability" of the trendline is significantly increased.

To draw an up trendline, we would look for a "locked in" MDRP UP. Then, we would draw the trendline from the close of the reference point (on the left) to the close of the MDRP UP (on the right) and extend the line to the right.

As a general rule, we are only concerned with where the close is in relationship to the trendline. This means that if prices are falling toward an up trendline, we would expect the Bulls to defend the trendline keeping the Bears from <u>closing</u> the bar below the trendline. Should the Bears close the bar below the up trendline, the trend is in jeopardy. Should the bar go below the trendline with the close being above it, we would not consider the uptrend to be in danger of failing.

As the timeframe of a chart increases, the significance of "N" closes under the up trendline increases. If we have drawn an up trendline based on an MDRP UP and the upside target has not been hit, the Bears closing the price below this line on a 5-minute chart is considerably less significant than if the trendline was drawn on a daily chart. The analogy is the same for the reliability of an MDRP UP or MDRP DOWN; a longer timeframe has more power and significance.

When a "locked in" Momentum Discrepancy Reversal Point is generated, a trendline using the correlated closing points can be drawn. Should this line be negated by a closing price, an early indication is given that the price target will NOT be met. When this occurs, we can exit the trade or move the protective stop.

CHAPTER 6

TREND DIRECTION USING MOMENTUM DISCREPANCY REVERSAL POINTS

When a Momentum Discrepancy Reversal Down (MDRP DOWN) forms, we know that the preceding trend has been down. We also know that prices are currently experiencing a retracement higher, if the prior trend was valid then the contra-trend retracement should end and the dominant trend should reassert itself. Momentum Discrepancy Reversals Down only occur in downtrends and Momentum Discrepancy Reversals Up only occur in uptrends. When we see one of these reversal patterns, we instantly know the probable trend direction.

DETERMINING TARGET LEVELS

When we see a Momentum Discrepancy Reversal Point, we can easily determine the upside or downside target that prices should hit. In fact, prices must hit the target if the preceding trend is still intact. These target prices are significant numbers. *If the target price is NOT exceeded on a closing basis, then the market is telling us that the current trend is finished.*

Upon seeing an MDRP UP, the upside target can be determined by obtaining the difference in price that coincides with the prior RSI trough and the current price. This difference is added to the intervening high close price giving us the upside target. The process is the same for determining downside target objectives. To determine an upside target, obtain the price that coincides with the two RSI troughs and add it to the highest close between these two troughs. To determine the downside target, obtain the closing price that coincides with the two RSI peaks and subtract this difference from the lowest close between these two peaks. These concepts were illustrated and previously discussed in the notes for Charts #17, #18 and #19.

THE MOST POWERFUL REVERSAL SIGNALS

The most powerful reversal signals occur when multiple timeframes with simultaneous reversal signals point in the same direction. If a 5-minute chart shows a Momentum Discrepancy Reversal Up, and a 30-minute chart simultaneously has a tentative Momentum Discrepancy Reversal Up, we have a very strong indication that the coming up move will be explosive. The Momentum Discrepancy Reversal Point signal becomes more significant as the length of the <u>timeframe</u> increases.

The second most powerful Momentum Discrepancy Reversal Point signal occurs when the time interval between the peaks or troughs is less than 5 bars. However, even long time intervals can result in powerful moves. Typically, if the time interval is more than 5 bars, we would like to see a price retracement that is less than 38.2%. This provides a very good indication that we will have a good up move and that the target price will be achieved. As the retracement level becomes deeper and the time period increases, it becomes less likely that the target price will be hit.

Of the many uses of the RSI, the MDRP Up or Down Reversals are the most powerful and profitable. The reversal signals tell us the direction of the trend, NOW is the time to enter the trade and the target price so we know where to exit the trade. By taking note of the corresponding price of the "locked in" MDRP UP or MDRP DOWN, we have a key price to work with. We also have another key price when we calculate the upside or downside target level.

Rule # 4
An Uptrend is indicated when:
1. RSI is in the 80/40 range
2. The chart shows simple bearish divergence
3. The chart shows Hidden bullish divergence
4. The chart shows Momentum Discrepancy Reversal Up

A Downtrend is indicated when:
1. RSI is in the 60/20 range
2. The chart shows simple bullish divergences.
3. The chart shows Hidden bearish divergence
4. The chart shows Momentum Discrepancy Reversal Down.

Chapter 7

The Relationship Between Price & RSI Retracements

As previously discussed, retracement moves are the result of traders becoming too emotional and pushing prices either too high or too low. When they realize that prices have been pushed to "hysterical levels," a contra-trend move commences where prices reverse and retrace some of the preceding move. The percentage that prices retrace a prior move is dependent upon the strength of the preceding trend, which is determined by the perception of the dominant traders.

We know that shallow retracements are less than 33%. Shallow retracements are a good indication that prices should extend higher by the same degree of the prior move. We also know that longer timeframe traders are either ignoring or agreeing with the price action, as the contra-trend move was less than 33% of the prior trend.

If a retracement of a rally in a 5-minute chart is hitting the 33% retracement level, and IF the 5-minute Bulls are in charge AND the longer timeframe traders (say the 15-minute traders) are asleep or in agreement with the prior rally, then we should see prices reverse higher <u>now</u>. The upside target is the same distance as the initial rally when calculated from the 33% retracement level. This was illustrated on page 26 in Table #9 of Section I.

We can use a similar line of reasoning with some modification when observing RSI behavior. Often, the RSI will show a shallow, medium, or deep retracement more distinctly than a price chart. We are not able to establish upside or downside target objectives using RSI retracement theory as we can with price retracement theory. For example, if the RSI rallies from 35 to 75, which is a move of 40 RSI points. If the RSI retraces 13 points to a value of 62, we know the retracement is shallow. Should there be no other timeframes in disagreement the RSI should rally to exceed its previous high. Unlike price, we cannot add 40 to 62 to obtain the upside RSI target of 102 because the RSI behaves as a logarithmic function with a maximum value of 100.

When attempting to combine price retracement theory with RSI retracement theory, we encounter some difficulties because the RSI can more easily overextend itself than price. This over-extension creates reversal formations such as MDRP UP and MDRP DOWN. Let's look at what typically happens when the RSI is <u>not overextending itself</u>.

Because the RSI is very sensitive to the movement of price especially in the 40 to 60 zone, it will usually retrace a larger percentage of its prior move than price. In other words, if price is retracing 33%, the RSI will often retrace 50 to 60%.

<u>Rules # 5 – General Rules of Retracements - Combined</u>

Price Retracement	RSI Retracement	Meaning
No more than 85.41%	approx. 125%	Momentum Discrepancy Reversal Point
~ 125% of previous leg up	61.80% to 85.41%	Bull Divergence
~ 125% of previous leg down	61.80% to 85.41%	Bear Divergence

We want to see a shallow <u>price</u> retracement coincide with a MDRP UP or MDRP DOWN. This provides two strong indications that the original trend will reassert itself with a shallow retracement and a Momentum Discrepancy Reversal Point. However, as the depth of the price retracement increases, the market is telling us that traders in a longer timeframe believe that the preceding trend was false, which gives them an opportunity to fade it. Should there be a "tentative" MDRP UP or MDRP DOWN concurrent with a medium or deep retracement, we should become cautious. As the percentage of the price retracement becomes deeper, the <u>probability</u> of achieving the target level obtained from the MDRP UP or MDRP DOWN begins to decrease. However, considering how the different timeframes interrelate, there are plenty of times, even with a deep retracement, that an MDRP UP or MDRP DOWN will easily surpass its upside or downside target level.

CHAPTER 8

IDENTIFYING SUPPORT AND RESISTANT PRICE LEVELS

We know that these are the 5 key numbers in order of importance:

1. The price where a Momentum Discrepancy Reversal Point is made
2. The upside or downside price target of a Momentum Discrepancy Reversal Point
3. The price where a basic retracement reverses (pages 18-20)
4. The price where a divergence occurs (using the right shoulder)

Now we have the ability to precisely identify important price levels, which allows us to set our stop levels. In the event they are hit, the trend has probably reversed or weakened so much that prices are about to stagnate. In either case, we really should no longer be in the trade.

Conventional knowledge states that the RSI chart is helpful in revealing certain price behaviors that are not so easily seen on a price chart. This is absolutely true once you understand the key numbers! At this point, you should have a thorough understanding of the RSI and be able to identify these important support and resistance levels.

The most important number is the Momentum Discrepancy Reversal Point price. Since the RSI is calculated on the closing price of a bar, stops can be placed tighter than using the low or high price. When day trading, I like to place stops 2 or 3 ticks away from these key prices. Since the charting application I use gives me the ability to enter text directly onto the chart, I enter the key numbers directly under the RSI patterns. This makes it very easy to identify key numbers and their locations.

CHART # 20 – TRADING CHART WITH PRICES ON RSI

Notes for Chart #20:

This is a chart that I use in trading. The only modification I made replacing the Candlesticks with bars for ease of printing. Since I use TradeStation™ Charting by Omega Research and Epsilon Charting, I have the ability to type the price just above the peak or trough on the RSI plus any comments I might have. I use the following color scheme:

1. Gray for bear or bull divergence.
2. Green for MDRP UP
3. Red for MDRP DOWN
4. Black for normal price

I also enter the target levels as T= "n" and any swing point greater than 1 as "s2," "s3," and so on depending upon strength. The colors used in the trendlines are the same as above.

On the far left of the chart is a bearish divergence at 1172.18 telling us that the market trend was UP. Prices fell to 1142.07 on March 25, which was below the support level at 40 RSI. At this point, we were not sure if the trend had definitely shifted, as it could have been nothing more than the 130-minute Bears and smaller timeframe traders becoming too pessimistic pushing prices lower before a timeframe longer than 130 minutes begins to buy. We don't have to wait long as prices rally to 1150.19 creating a MDRP DOWN. We know that the Bears have once again re-asserted themselves at this point. They confirm their strength by closing prices below the downside target of 1138.17 at 1134.85 just 3 bars later! After studying the RSI to this point, you should be able to place a piece of paper over the price action and tell by the RSI chart everything we originally set out to accomplish as outlined on page 4 in Section I.

End chart # 20 notes.

CHAPTER 9

HELP! A LONGER TIMEFRAME JUMPED IN MY PUDDLE!

We know that the marketplace consists of traders who focus the majority of their energies on different timeframes primarily because of their level of capitalization. At times, different timeframes will be the reason for the underlying price momentum. The concept of trading in different timeframes is a very difficult concept to fully understand and is considerably beyond the scope of this book. For the purposes of this book, all we need to understand is when the timeframe we are focusing on has been taken over (permanently or temporarily) by a different timeframe.

This is easy to determine using Momentum Discrepancy Reversal Points and divergence. For example, if we see that prices are steadily falling on a 30-minute S&P chart. Then, we see a small contra-trend rally of less than 32% before the market once again falls to new lows. This decline is followed by another contra-trend rally. This time the contra-trend move rallies almost 50% on the price chart and 105% on the RSI chart giving us an MDRP DOWN. Once again prices eventually fall and exceed the targeted low. This is a good example of a solid bear market that is controlled primarily by the 30-minute traders in agreement with shorter and longer-term traders – i.e., prices and RSI perform as expected.

However, what happens if the 450-minute traders decide that the move down should be faded because they think prices are going higher without letting the 30-minute traders know? These traders begin to buy on weakness to reduce slippage. This means that we will see the formation of multiple bullish divergences. More importantly, the market will be unable to achieve the targeted lows created by any future MDRP DOWN! Without knowing that it is the 450-minute traders who are fading our 30-minute bear party, we <u>must</u> as 30-minute traders recognize the clues. There are simple and multiple divergences and failed MDRP DOWN targets. Upon recognizing the clues, we can either exit our short positions or tighten our stops until we are stopped out of our positions. When the 30-minute timeframe traders are once again in charge, we can re-enter the marketplace in the direction of the 30-minute chart.

If we are interested in aligning our trade position with the dominant traders, we must examine multiple timeframes until we find a timeframe where the price behavior becomes crystal clear. In our example, once we look at a 450-minute chart, we might discover that the reason the 450-minute traders faded the 30-minute bear market was because there was a MDRP UP or perhaps even a long-term bear divergence on the 450-minute chart!

In summary, we know that longer timeframe traders have decided to enter the game when what should be working – fails. The market is indicating something significant when there is a "high probability expectation" that fails. You must be paying attention at all times. We can also identify when shorter timeframe traders have decided to play because they are the ones that create the MDRP UP and MDRP DOWN formations. They are also the reason that the 60 and 40 levels are slightly exceeded in a bear or bull market respectively.

CHAPTER 10

CONCLUSION

Now we have a working model of how price and RSI behave and relate. We have also discussed why there are different timeframe traders and how these traders interrelate with each other. We have studied basic retracement theory, the different types of divergences and their meanings and Momentum Discrepancy Reversal Points.

To successfully use everything requires a trader to have a thorough understanding of the underlying principles. The foundation of this working model is the mathematics of the RSI calculation and Fibonacci ratios. The mathematics tells us that there is a certain zone where the RSI is most comfortable. It is in this zone that very slight changes in price are easily magnified, and RSI values where price changes barely move the RSI value. The Fibonacci number sequence allows us to identify percentage retracement levels that will help us identify the strength or weakness of a preceding trend.

The real nature of the marketplace is one where any two traders can agree upon a price and this price can be valid or invalid depending upon whether one trader was "forced" to trade. In this case, the information that the "trade price" conveys is worthless. We learned that because of the different capitalization levels of traders, not all traders are focused on the same interval of time. We also know that simple divergences are a good way to quickly determine the trend and when we see a divergence, we should begin looking for a place to fade the coming contra-trend move.

Often, the place or price to fade this retracement move is when we see an MDRP DOWN or MDRP UP in the RSI that coincides with a shallow to medium retracement in price. Once we have a "tentative" MDRP UP or MDRP DOWN, we can determine the upside or downside price target. Once this MDRP DOWN or UP becomes "locked in," we have a valid support or resistance price that we can be used for our stop placement. Using the targeted upside or downside price, we have a place to confidently take some or all of our profits.

If the targeted price is not reached, the trend is probably about to end. An early indication that the price objective is in danger is the negation of a corresponding trendline on a closing basis by one or more bars depending upon the timeframe being used. We also know that we can determine when longer-term timeframe traders are present because the targeted level is not achieved and/or we begin seeing multiple signal divergences. We can also detect short-term traders because they typically create the MDRP UP and MDRP DOWN formations and cause the 40 support and 60 resistance levels to occasionally be exceeded in bull and bear markets. By identifying the prices that create the RSI patterns, we are able to use those price levels as stops allowing us to capture additional profits. Here is a summary of everything:

TREND DETERMINATION TABLE

Uptrend	Downtrend
1. RSI ranges from 80/40	1. RSI ranges from 60/20
2. Simple Bearish Divergence	2. Simple Bullish Divergence
3. Hidden Bullish Divergence	3. Hidden Bearish Divergence
4. Momentum Discrepancy Reversal Up	4. Momentum Discrepancy Reversal Down
5. Upside Targets being hit.	5. Downside Targets being hit.
6. 9 bar simple moving average is greater than the 45 bar exponential moving average on RSI	6. 9 bar simple moving average is less than the 45 bar exponential moving average on RSI
7. Contra-trend declines do not exceed 50% of previous rally	7. Contra-trends rallies do not exceed 50% of previous decline

TREND IN DANGER TABLE

Uptrend in Danger	Downtrend in Danger
1. Longer Timeframe fading rally	1. Longer timeframe fading decline
2. a. Multiple long-term bearish divergences b. Upside targets not being hit.	2. a. Multiple long-term bullish divergences. b. Upside targets not being hit.
3. 9 bar simple moving average less than the 45 bar exponential moving average on RSI	3. 9 bar simple moving average greater than the 45 bar exponential moving average on RSI
4. Hidden Bearish Divergence, or simple Bullish Divergence	4. Hidden Bullish Divergence, or simple Bearish Divergence
5. Deep contra-trend retracements	5. Deep contra-trend retracements

Appendix A

Day	Close	Change	Advance	Decline	AvgGain	AvgLoss	RS	Close
	1380.47							
1	1380.42	=B3-B2	=B3-B2	=IF(OR(C3<0,C3=0),ABS(C3),0)				
2	1380.71	=B4-B3	=B4-B3	=IF(OR(C4<0,C4=0),ABS(C4),0)				
3	1380.74	=B5-B4	=B5-B4	=IF(OR(C5<0,C5=0),ABS(C5),0)				
4	1380.88	=B6-B5	=B6-B5	=IF(OR(C6<0,C6=0),ABS(C6),0)				
5	1380.74	=B7-B6	=B7-B6	=IF(OR(C7<0,C7=0),ABS(C7),0)				
6	1380.53	=B8-B7	=B8-B7	=IF(OR(C8<0,C8=0),ABS(C8),0)				
7	1381.01	=B9-B8	=B9-B8	=IF(OR(C9<0,C9=0),ABS(C9),0)				
8	1381.07	=B10-B9	=B10-B9	=IF(OR(C10<0,C10=0),ABS(C10),0)				
9	1381.48	=B11-B10	=B11-B10	=IF(OR(C11<0,C11=0),ABS(C11),0)				
10	1382.19	=B12-B11	=B12-B11	=IF(OR(C12<0,C12=0),ABS(C12),0)				
11	1382.08	=B13-B12	=B13-B12	=IF(OR(C13<0,C13=0),ABS(C13),0)				
12	1382.05	=B14-B13	=B14-B13	=IF(OR(C14<0,C14=0),ABS(C14),0)				
13	1382.09	=B15-B14	=B15-B14	=IF(OR(C15<0,C15=0),ABS(C15),0)				
14	1381.95	=B16-B15	=B16-B15	=IF(OR(C16<0,C16=0),ABS(C16),0)	=AVERAGE(D3:D16)	=AVERAGE(E3:E16)	=ABS(F16/G16)	=100-(100/(1+H16))
15	1382.18	=B17-B16	=B17-B16	=IF(OR(C17<0,C17=0),ABS(C17),0)	=((F16*13)+D17)/14	=((G16*13)+E17)/14	=ABS(F17/G17)	=100-(100/(1+H17))
16	1382.22	=B18-B17	=B18-B17	=IF(OR(C18<0,C18=0),ABS(C18),0)	=((F17*13)+D18)/14	=((G17*13)+E18)/14	=ABS(F18/G18)	=100-(100/(1+H18))
17	1382.12	=B19-B18	=B19-B18	=IF(OR(C19<0,C19=0),ABS(C19),0)	=((F18*13)+D19)/14	=((G18*13)+E19)/14	=ABS(F19/G19)	=100-(100/(1+H19))
18	1382.36	=B20-B19	=B20-B19	=IF(OR(C20<0,C20=0),ABS(C20),0)	=((F19*13)+D20)/14	=((G19*13)+E20)/14	=ABS(F20/G20)	=100-(100/(1+H20))
19	1382.32	=B21-B20	=B21-B20	=IF(OR(C21<0,C21=0),ABS(C21),0)	=((F20*13)+D21)/14	=((G20*13)+E21)/14	=ABS(F21/G21)	=100-(100/(1+H21))
20	1382.22	=B22-B21	=B22-B21	=IF(OR(C22<0,C22=0),ABS(C22),0)	=((F21*13)+D22)/14	=((G21*13)+E22)/14	=ABS(F22/G22)	=100-(100/(1+H22))
21	1382.15	=B23-B22	=B23-B22	=IF(OR(C23<0,C23=0),ABS(C23),0)	=((F22*13)+D23)/14	=((G22*13)+E23)/14	=ABS(F23/G23)	=100-(100/(1+H23))
22	1382.22	=B24-B23	=B24-B23	=IF(OR(C24<0,C24=0),ABS(C24),0)	=((F23*13)+D24)/14	=((G23*13)+E24)/14	=ABS(F24/G24)	=100-(100/(1+H24))
23	1382.12	=B25-B24	=B25-B24	=IF(OR(C25<0,C25=0),ABS(C25),0)	=((F24*13)+D25)/14	=((G24*13)+E25)/14	=ABS(F25/G25)	=100-(100/(1+H25))

Use these formulas to construct a 14 period RSI

To build a 3 period RSI eliminate lines 3, 4, 5, 6, 7, 8, 9, 10, 11, 12, 13

Appendix B
TREND DETERMINATION— A QUICK, ACCURATE & EFFECTIVE METHODOLOGY
By John Hayden

This short article was written for my clients and friends in the spring of 2000. It is included here to help those that are interested in understanding how the RSI can be incorporated into an overall trading strategy. I have modified it to eliminate any redundancy with the majority of this book.

It is my belief that it is a valid indicator that will work in all markets and all time frames. The RSI can be used for:

1. Trend Analysis
2. Determining Price Objectives

After reading and studying the material within this book you should have a through understanding of the RSI. At this point we will broaden our examination of some other momentum based indicators.

Momentum derived oscillators are very popular among futures traders and have become increasingly popular among stock traders.

The first momentum indicator measures the change in the closing price over 'N' units of time. This indicator is referred to as the Momentum Indicator and it measures the absolute change in price by calculating

(Present Price)-(Price 'N' Time Periods Ago)

The second momentum indicator is called the Rate of Change Indicator, which measures relative change by the formula,

(Present Price)/(Price 'N' Time Periods Ago)

The third momentum-derived oscillator is the Stochastic Indicator developed by George Lane. This indicator measures the relationship between the closing price and the high and low price for the time period under consideration. The formula is

[(Present Closing Price – Lowest Low 'N' Time Periods Ago)/(Highest High 'N' Time Periods Ago – Lowest Low 'N' Time Periods Ago)] * 100

This formula is a more involved than the simple Momentum Indicator formula.

The fourth momentum-derived oscillator is the Relative Strength Index (RSI), which we have described in depth.

With the first three oscillators, Momentum, Rate of Change, and Stochastic, a major problem occurs when large price movements are dropped from the calculation during the time period under consideration. This causes the indicator to oscillate more frequently and with an larger amplitude than it should.

For example, here is a chart of the March 2000 Silver contract where we look at two consecutive days for the Rate of Change and Momentum indicators.

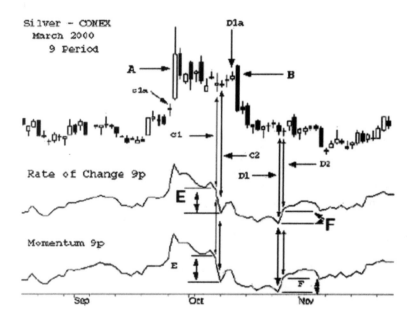

In early October, Silver had a large one-day advance (A) at C1. When the 9-period Rate of Change or Momentum Indicator is calculated, the calculation is based upon the closing price at (C1a) with the current closing price at (C1). The next day (C2), shows a closing price that is barely changed from (C1). However when the calculations are redone using the closing price of (A) and the closing price of (C2), the large up move is dropped and the value of the Rate of Change and the Momentum Indicator makes a large move as measured by (E) while the price at (C1 & C2) have barely changed! This problem can also be observed in conjunction with the large down move (B).

Observe what happens when we change the look back period to 10 days. Immediately, we notice that the large moves at (A) and (B) are still included in the look back that is calculated on the second day.

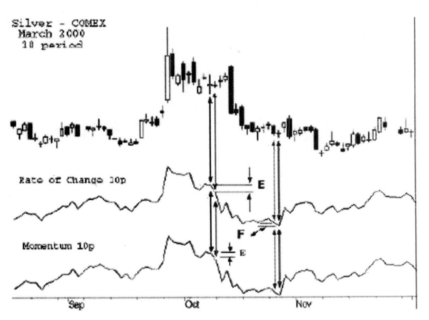

As shown by the chart, the amount that the oscillator changed (E) and (F) is much less when the look back period is extended to 10 days because the oscillator for both days is looking at the price before the large move. The oscillators continue to drop at (F), where in the 9-day look back, the oscillators actually increased in value. It is interesting that the price of silver actually dropped a tenth of a cent on this day! This is a major problem when using these simple momentum oscillators.

Because of its construction, the RSI dampens or smoothes these distortions. Here are the same charts with a 9-day and 10-day look back period of the RSI.

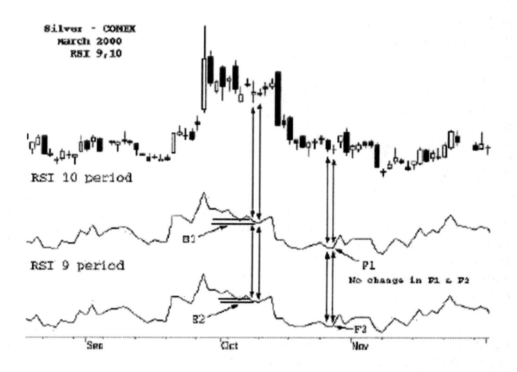

The vertical distance the RSI value moves (E1 vs. E2) and (F1 vs. F2) remains basically the same if the large moves are included or not included. This allows us to place more significance on the actual values of the RSI. The Relative Strength Index is always contained within a vertical range that runs from 0 to 100. This saves us the trouble of constantly referring to past indicator values when determining overbought or oversold levels. This problem occurs because typical momentum indicators values are not contained within a predefined vertical range.

When discussing the RSI, most books on technical analysis typically use a 14-day look back period for their calculation. It should be noted that a longer look back period makes a less sensitive RSI oscillation. When a smaller look back period is used, the amplitude of the oscillation increases. I prefer to use a look back period of 14 days or time periods. This look back works best in all time frames and is one half the lunar cycle for daily data.

For intra-day time frames, some traders use a 9-period look back. In gold, silver, crude oil and the financial markets, a 25-day look back period performs well. There seems to be a 50-day cycle in these markets and a 25-day look back is half the cycle length. It is important to realize that the Relative Strength Index formula requires at least 90 time periods of data to provide valid results. Otherwise, the formula will not yield accurate results for trend analysis. When I look at daily charts, I prefer to have at least 200 days of data to trust the validity of the RSI data.

An important fact to remember is that any oscillator, the RSI included, will become either overbought (bull market) or oversold (bear market) in a strongly trending market. Consequently, the momentum indicator or oscillator will remain oversold or overbought for quite a while.

DETERMINING THE RSI RANGE

An up trending market will typically find support at the RSI value 40 with effective resistance at the RSI value 80. A down trending market will find resistance at RSI value 60 with effective support at RSI value 20. Often, a primary indication that the trend has shifted from bearish to a possible bull market occurs when the RSI that previously respected the 60 level rallies up to an RSI value of 70 or higher. When the inevitable decline occurs, the RSI will respect the RSI value 40 before rallying again.

In an 80/40 range (bull market), you will see the RSI make higher highs and higher bottoms, which is a classic indication of a bull market! Similarly, in a 60/20 range (bear market), you will see the RSI making lower lows and lower tops. Recognizing this RSI behavior is very useful when looking at a futures or stock chart. Inspecting the range that the RSI is moving in provides the first clue that indicates the trend direction. The RSI finds resistance or support at previous tops and/or bottoms in the RSI values themselves. Old resistance points can become new resistance points and if broken, become a new support level upon a retracement. Old support levels can prove to be effective support again and, if broken, prove to be effective resistance.

Here is a longer term Japanese Yen chart:

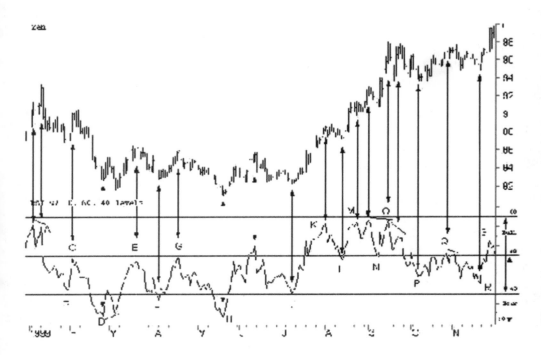

At (A) there is a small bearish divergence indicating that the prior uptrend is about to take a detour. Prices decline to (B) where the market finds support at the RSI 40 level. The rally to (C) is the first hint that a trend change could be coming, as the RSI 60 level proves to be effective resistance. The decline in prices to (D) violates the previous support line at 40. At this point, it becomes apparent that what should have been support has failed. RSI value 60 was effective resistance at (C) and these two elements combined point to the fact that the trend has probably changed. The price rallies a bit after (D) before faltering and declining to a new low. However, the RSI value fails to make a new low. Instead, it makes a bullish divergence! At this point, we can safely say that the previous bull market has died! Our opinion is strengthened with the RSI level of 60 at (C) proving to be resistance and the 40 level failing to provide support in the decline from (C) to (D) plus a bullish divergence. The point where the Bulls got excited about the bullish divergence is where we should be looking for a place to get short!

The rally to (E) respects the RSI 60 level before dropping to (F). However, the RSI does find some support at (F). This indicates that the Bulls might be preparing to rally prices. When the rally falters at (G), we can safely assume that the bear market is still in effect. The low at (H) was not followed by a bullish divergence, which is a minor indication that a trend change could be coming. This was confirmed to some degree at (I) when the RSI managed to rally above 60 to 64.93 before dropping back. Our suspicions became more valid as the decline to (J) found support at the RSI 40 level. This was similar to the RSI finding resistance at the 60 level at (C). The rally to (K) violated the RSI 60 resistance level. The decline at (L) which found support at the RSI 60 level confirmed that we were back in a bull market. In fact, just as we were looking for a place to get short the market prior to (E), we should now be looking for a place to get long prior to (L). Remember, the RSI tends to find support (L) at old resistance levels (C, E, G, H) in a bull market.

In any case, the rally to (M) met resistance at the RSI 80 level. The subsequent decline to (N) found support at the RSI 60 level. Notice that this is the second time that the RSI 60 level has acted as support. This behavior by the RSI indicates that we are in a strong bull market. This would be similar to the RSI 40 level acting as resistance in a bear market. In fact, after the bear decline to (D), the market rallied a bit finding resistance at the 40 level six days later (a six-period bullish divergence).

Following the rally from (N), there was a bearish divergence at (O), followed by another divergence a few days later. The decline in prices to (P) was followed by a warning that the trend could be changing, which came at (Q) as the RSI found resistance at the 60 level with a small bearish divergence that led to a decline to (R). The explosive rally to (S) provided a strong indication that the bull market was still alive and well.

It is interesting to note that (S) is a longer-term bearish divergence against (O). The first indication by the RSI that the bull market in Yen has ended will be the 60 level acting as resistance followed by a violation of the 40 level – or the price negating the 40 support level without first encountering resistance at the 60 level.

DETERMINING SUPPORT & RESISTANCE LEVELS

It is important to look for support and resistance levels on both the price and RSI charts. I look at the RSI chart to determine at what price and at what level the RSI found effective resistance and support. In an up trending market, the charts reveal that current support levels were former resistance levels on the price and RSI chart during previous days and weeks. In a down trending market, the charts reveal that the price or RSI values will eventually violate former support levels. As a result, these former support levels were transformed into current resistance levels by the down trending market behavior.

LOOKING FOR A DIVERGENCE

A very significant clue that the trend is changing occurs when a divergence is present. A possible bullish divergence occurs when the price makes a new low, but the momentum oscillator fails to also make a new low. It becomes a valid bullish divergence when the price turns up from the low and the oscillator also turns up. A possible bearish divergence occurs when price makes a new high, but the RSI fails to make a new high. It becomes a valid bearish divergence when the price drops.

I hinted at this in the above section. What I am about to say next will shock traditional traders. Whenever I see a bearish divergence, I immediately start to think that we are in a *BULL* market. Whenever I see a bullish divergence, I start to think that we are in a *BEAR* market! I know that this flies in the face of what the textbooks say. Remember, as traders, we want to detect the moment the market might change its direction. The important point is that in the *majority* of the cases, my claim is very true.

You will find repeated bearish divergences only in an uptrending market. Similarly, bullish divergences will only repeatedly occur in a bearish market. If you find this hard to accept, find a chart (weekly, daily) of the Japanese Yen, and start looking at what the RSI did from July 7, 1995 to July 7, 1998. You will be hard pressed to find a bearish divergence in the daily chart and there is no bearish divergence in the weekly chart! Detecting a divergence is one of my favorite tools.

This next chart displays how stock prices and futures prices behave the same. Notice how the 80/40 RSI levels were respected by multiple bearish divergences, but no bullish divergences! The CISCO stock experienced multiple Bearish Divergences and the price continued to rally. Bearish Divergence usually occurs in a BULL MARKET!

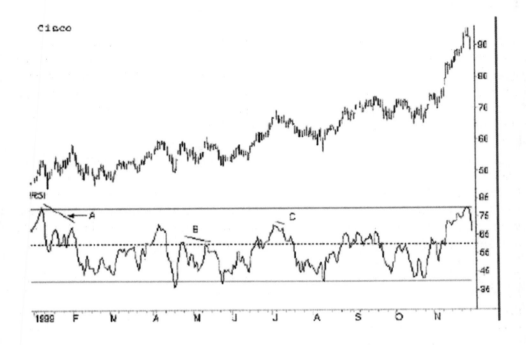

Think of a divergence as a detour. The overall trend will resume once the price gets past this temporary resistance or support area. Divergences are always associated with momentum-based indicators and typically shows up at the momentum high or low. For example when a bull market is overbought, there will be a correction. Before the correction, there will be a loss of market momentum. When a bearish divergence occurs, the market is telling you that it is overbought or overextended. When this occurs, you might want to take partial profits on your long position, because prices could be preparing to take a detour! Remember that the bearish divergence that occurs during the bull market is not telling you to get short!

Cisco Stock

A divergence takes a certain number of days to form. The strength of a divergence is based on the length of the formation time period. Calculate the period of a divergence as follows: the above Cisco stock chart prices have been advancing into late April (A), making a high close at 'x'. The price and RSI are both making new highs (A). For the next 8 days, both price and RSI drop with neither going higher than the previous value at 'x'. Following this decline, both price and RSI reverse direction and rally for four days. At the close of the fourth day of this short rally, the price is higher than it was 12 days earlier at 'x'. But, the RSI is still lower than its previous peak. Consequently, there may be 12-day divergence during the 2nd week of May.

At this time, it is a possible or 'tentative divergence' because to become a 'locked in divergence,' the price has to drop. It is the dropping price that will prevent the RSI value from exceeding 'x', and will "hook" the RSI over or turn the RSI value down, making the divergence real. It is important to remember that until the RSI value actually drops under its previous value, this remains a 'tentative divergence' because the RSI value could exceed the 'x' value if prices continue up negating the divergence. This means that we must wait one day or one period of time to confirm a valid divergence according to the definition.

Our next example (B) shows a 4-period divergence. The duration of a divergence is important. A two to six day divergence usually indicates that a detour in price is more likely than a longer period. A longer divergence period of weeks and even months, if using daily charts, is usually less indicative that a price detour is coming. The most powerful divergence occurs during a 2 or 3 period divergence. In the overall context of RSI applications as a trading tool, the divergence signals are relatively minor. I enjoy using divergence to detect what the overall trend is. Divergence is very useful in deciding where to take partial profits in multiple contract positions.

USING MOVING AVERAGES

Another tool that I use to indicate trend is moving averages. This is the standard workhorse tool used by most technical traders. Moving averages are valuable because they remove the volatility from the data series. For example, calculating a moving average based on the RSI effectively removes the volatility from the RSI calculation and yields a smoother signal. In fact, the trend can be confirmed by calculating a 9-period simple moving average (SMA) and a 45-period weighted moving average (WMA) on the RSI and price. When the:

1.   The 9-period on price is above the 45-period on price, and
      the 9-period on RSI is above the 45-period on RSI the trend is *up*.
2.   The 9-period on price is below the 45-period on price, and
      the 9-period on RSI is below the 45-period on RSI the trend is *down*.
3.   The 9 period on price is above the 45 period on price, and
      the 9-period on RSI is below the 45-period on RSI the trend is
      sideways to up.
4.   The 9-period on price is below the 45-period on price, and
      the 9-period on RSI is above the 45-period on RSI the trend is
      sideways to down.

Since the RSI is more volatile than price, the 9-period simple moving average (SMA) of the RSI will cross its respective 45-period weighted moving average (WMA) before the 9-period moving average (SMA) on price will cross its respective 45-period moving average (WMA). I place more emphasis on the moving averages based on price than those based on RSI. By remaining aware of what the moving averages are doing will help you to stay focused on the overall trend. When I am talking to another trader, I will often say that the moving average on price is positive. This implies that the short-term 9-period SMA is above the longer-term 45-period WMA. The largest moves frequently occur when both moving averages are moving in the same direction.

One more thought on moving averages. You will find that the 45-period weighted moving average (WMA) will prove to be support or resistance on price and the RSI. For example, you will often see a bull market retrace to its respective 45-period weighted moving average in price and/or RSI. When this is observed it is another sign of what the trend actually is.

Here is an example of the U.S Treasury 30-Year Treasury Bond:

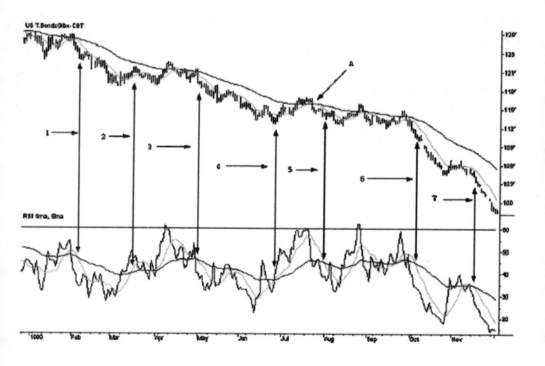

From looking at this chart, it is obvious that the trend had been down since the beginning of 1999. However, by applying the previously discussed rules, we can see the following. At (1) with the close at: 124^14, the price found resistance at the 45-period moving average (the red line). Also, notice that the 9-period moving average (the green line) on the RSI crossed under the 45-period moving average resuming the downtrend. At point (2) (122^09), the trend changed to 'sideways to down' preventing us from looking for a place to get long. Instead, it forced us to look for a place to get short.

This became obvious at point (3) (120^04), where the trend went back to 'down.' The trend shifted back to 'sideways to up' at point (4) (114^20). After the rally to (A), many traders began to believe that the price would continue higher. At (A), several things occurred. First, the trend was up, as the moving average on price and the RSI were positive. Second, the RSI was unable to overcome the RSI 60-resistance level. Third, the price is not able to distance itself from the 45-period moving average on price. This is indicating that the probable direction of price would remain down. Moreover, the decline into early August showed that the RSI broke possible support at 40, indicating probable lower prices.

At (6) (111^03), the trend turned down again. Between points 5 (114^26) and 6 (111^03), the moving average went positive and negative a couple times. However, notice that the RSI continued to respect the 60-resistance level and the moving average on price continued to be negative. Then, at point (6) (111^03), the trend resumed its downward trend. At point (7) (103^19), the trend briefly went 'sideways to down.' This was a false move because the RSI was finding resistance at the RSI 40 level. The fact that the RSI 40 level had acted as support in late August was also significant. Remember that in a bear market, what was support will often become resistance on a subsequent rally. This was signifying the probability of a major downward move in price.

In conclusion, the questions that I ask myself when determining trend are:
1. What is the RSI range?
2. Has there been a range shift?
3. Is the market respecting its former support and resistance areas?
4. Is the market violating support and resistance areas and reversing their roles?
5. Have prices broken important trendlines in the price or RSI chart?
6. What type of divergence is present?
7. What is my moving averages showing me?

This quick checklist is how I can accurately and quickly determine the trend. My book *The 21 Irrefutable Truths of Trading – A Traders Guide To Developing A Mind To Win* (McGraw-Hill, 2000) provides more in-depth technical analysis methodologies to determine trend, when to enter and exit a trade and the psychological characteristics that successful traders possess. You can order this book at Traders Press, Inc., PO Box 6206, Greenville, SC 29606 ~ http://www.traderspress.com ~ 800-927-8222 ~ 864-298-0222 ~ fax 864-298-0221.

Appendix C

Examples of longer term charts:

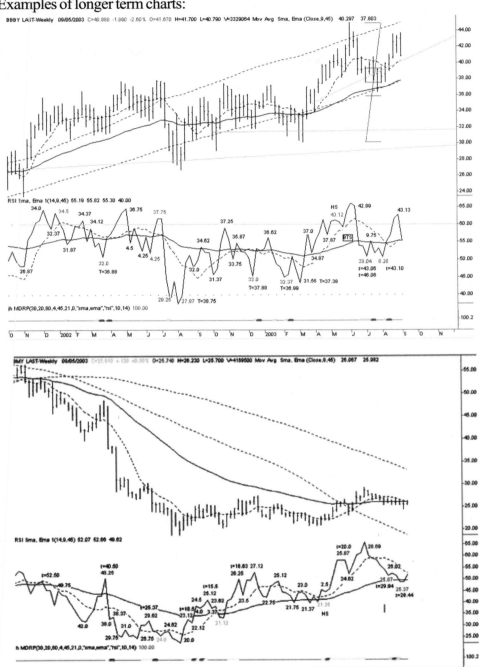

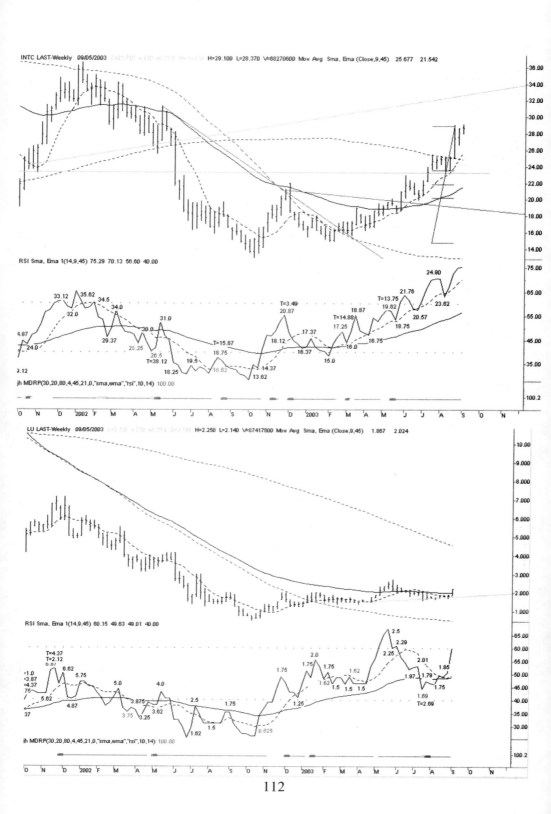

ORCL LAST-Weekly 09/05/2003 C=13.080 -.640 -4.66% O=13.400 H=13.510 L=13.000 V=77520512 Mov Avg Sma, Ema (Close,9,45) 12.262 11.993

RSI Sma, Ema 1(14,9,45) 57.74 51.63 52.26 40.00

jr. MDRP(30,20,80,4,45,21,0,"sma,wma","rsi",10,14) 100.00

Appendix D

John Hayden lives in Samara, Russia and is easily contacted by email:
jhayden@FirstVolgaInvestments.com.
His website is: **www.FirstVolgaInvestments.com.**

The charts used in this book were created with **EpsilonCharting**. This is a charting program that Mr. Hayden is developing for professional traders.

ished by: Traders Press, Inc.®

7 Secrets Every Commodity Trader Needs to Know (Mound)
A Complete Guide to Trading Profits (Paris)
A Professional Look at S&P Day Trading (Trivette)
A Treasury of Wall Street Wisdom (Editors: Schultz & Coslow)
Ask Mr. EasyLanguage (Tennis)
Beginner's Guide to Computer Assisted Trading (Alexander)
Channels and Cycles: A Tribute to J.M. Hurst (Millard)
Chart Reading for Professional Traders (Jenkins)
Commodity Spreads: Analysis, Selection and Trading Techniques (Smith)
Comparison of Twelve Technical Trading Systems (Lukac, Brorsen, & Irwin)
Complete Stock Market Trading and Forecasting Course (Jenkins)
Cyclic Analysis (J.M. Hurst)
Dynamic Trading (Miner)
Exceptional Trading: The Mind Game (Roosevelt)
Fibonacci Ratios with Pattern Recognition (Pesavento)
Futures Spread Trading: The Complete Guide (Smith)
Geometry of Markets (Gilmore)
Geometry of Stock Market Profits (Jenkins)
Harmonic Vibrations (Pesavento)
How to Trade in Stocks (Livermore & Smitten)
Hurst Cycles Course (J.M. Hurst)
Investing by the Stars (Weingarten)
Investor Skills Training: Managing Emotions and Risk in the Market (Ronin)
It's Your Option (Zelkin)
Magic of Moving Averages (Lowry)
Market Rap: The Odyssey of a Still-Struggling Commodity Trader (Collins)
Overcoming 7 Deadly Sins of Trading (Roosevelt)
Planetary Harmonics of Speculative Markets (Pesavento)
Point & Figure Charting (Aby)
Point & Figure Charting: Commodity and Stock Trading Techniques (Zieg)
Private Thoughts From a Trader's Diary (Pesavento & MacKay)
Profitable Patterns for Stock Trading (Pesavento)
RoadMap to the Markets (Busby)
Short-Term Trading with Price Patterns (Harris)
Single Stock Futures: The Complete Guide (Greenberg)
Stock Patterns for Day Trading (2 volumes) (Rudd)
Stock Trading Techniques Based on Price Patterns (Harris)
Technically Speaking (Wilkinson)
Technical Trading Systems for Commodities and Stocks (Patel)
The Amazing Life of Jesse Livermore: World's Greatest Stock Trader (Smitten)
The Handbook of Global Securities Operations (O'Connell & Steiniger)
The Opening Price Principle: The Best Kept Secret on Wall Street (Pesavento & MacKay)
The Professional Commodity Trader (Kroll)
The Taylor Trading Technique (Taylor)
The Trading Rule That Can Make You Rich* (Dobson)
Top Traders Under Fire (Collins)
Trading Secrets of the Inner Circle (Goodwin)
Trading S&P Futures and Options (Lloyd)
Twelve Habitudes of Highly Successful Traders (Roosevelt)
Understanding Bollinger Bands (Dobson)
Understanding Eminis: Trading to Win (Williams)
Understanding Fibonacci Numbers (Dobson)
Viewpoints of a Commodity Trader (Longstreet)
Winning Edge 4 (Toghraie)
Winning Market Systems (Appel)

**Please contact Traders Press to receive our current catalog describing these and
many other books and gifts of interest to investors and traders.**
800-927-8222 ~ 864-298-0222 ~ fax 864-298-0221
http://www.traderspress.com ~ e-mail ~ customerservice@traderspress.com